Baseball in
HUNTSVILLE

Baseball in HUNTSVILLE

MARK McCARTER

THE
History
PRESS

Published by The History Press
Charleston, SC
www.historypress.com

Front cover, top left: Huntsville-Madison County Public Library Special Collection; *top right*: courtesy Huntsville Public Library; *bottom*: courtesy Rocket City Trash Pandas.
Back cover, top left: Alabama Media Group; *top right*: courtesy Alabama Media Group.

First published 2023

Manufactured in the United States

ISBN 9781467152693

Library of Congress Control Number: 2022948308

To the memory of Don Mincher, Huntsville's Mr. Baseball, and to the General, John Pruett, the ranking officer of all Huntsville journalists.

CONTENTS

ACKNOWLEDGEMENTS

$\mathcal{A}$s with too many things in this stage of our history, COVID-19 is to blame. I had reported, researched and written a book on the arrival of the Rocket City Trash Pandas. The week it was to print, the COVID shutdown began. Once that book took on a different shape, it made superfluous an extensive amount of research and writing about Huntsville's rich baseball history. Thus, my first acknowledgement and thanks go to Joe Gartrell of Arcadia/The History Press, who championed the effort to bring that work into print.

Other thanks go, as always, to my wife, Patricia, who encouraged this project and others. Thanks also to Bob Ludwig, a writer's publisher, and Joe Distelheim, a writer's editor, at the *Huntsville Times*, who facilitated my coverage of the Stars and so much else. Thanks also to coworkers at papers in Chattanooga, Anniston and Huntsville and the fellow travelers with whom I shared so many press boxes. And maybe most important, thanks to a high school friend named Jan Belk, who noted that the Brainerd High School *Reveille*, for which she served as editor, needed a sportswriter. It was there that the first keystrokes from the asdfghjkl; line led to this bit of work.

BRINGING BASEBALL TO HUNTSVILLE

LIKE LANDING A MAN ON THE MOON

*T*here was barely enough time.

There was too much time.

With that Dickensian spin, two red-letter dates on a century-plus timeline of professional baseball in the Huntsville area are defined. One involves a hurry-up stadium design and construction, in which local lore would have you believe that sign painters and contractors were spinning out of the turnstiles on one side as eager fans were pouring in on the other. The second touches on a magnificent new stadium forced to sit empty as a worldwide pandemic changed our lives and left 2020 as a gloomy year of social distancing and canceled sports.

Between those mileposts were more than two thousand Huntsville Stars games at Joe W. Davis Stadium and six years without a team the area could call its own. The Stars era comprised three decades marked by the emergence of inflated players who'd post inflated statistics, a dedicated local ownership, three pennants, a home-grown MVP, an apathetic long-distance ownership, inattentive landlord-ship and skunks in the outfield that would inspire a mascot (as opposed to another furry and pesky mascot that labeled a whole roster in the next iteration of pro ball).

Before the first milepost were three other professional baseball debuts, dating to 1903, each seemingly more ill-advised than the other. Each came with extravagant hype and hubbub, whether it be pandering to female fans, tsunamis of civic pride, mayoral proclamations, gushing editorials or the

Toyota Field became home to the Rocket City Trash Pandas in the 2021 season. *Courtesy Rocket City Trash Pandas.*

sobering notion that a team would pat itself on the back by welcoming Black patrons to their own special, segregated viewing section.

When pro baseball was first launched, Huntsville was a small, cotton-smothered speck on the map, no larger or more formidable than other Alabama burgs like Talladega and Selma and that archrival across the Tennessee River, Decatur. As the cotton industry grew, such was the impact of the rival mills that a Huntsville pro baseball team couldn't compete at the box office—or even on the field—with the mill-league amateur teams.

That bunch of pros, the Huntsville Springers, finished a miserable 35-66 in 1933. More than one baseball writer could feel the pain of an anonymous scribe in the *Huntsville Daily News* who groused, "Ho-hum, it makes one tired and disgusted to just have to write about it."

It would be another fifty years before anyone had reason to write about a professional baseball team in north Alabama.

Then came April 19, 1985, with the Huntsville Stars' home debut against the Birmingham Barons. It was described as "the most exciting thing that has happened to Huntsville since man landed on the moon." That, from Huntsville City Council member John Glenn, a man who doubtless for years lugged around the parenthetical phrase "no relation to," sharing a name with the iconic astronaut and future senator who was an occasional visitor to the Huntsville and Redstone Arsenal.

As Stars' management would bemoan through the years, an essentially eight-month window in which to design and construct a twelve-thousand-seat stadium was a tight squeeze. Shortcuts and budget left things incomplete. The rapid process didn't allow for enough foresight to imagine the growing demands of minor-league teams and fans.

It also didn't allow proper time to cultivate a field. The Stars' first home run in the infant park, to ignite a 10–0 win over Birmingham, was an inside-the-park job when a bad hop on a Ray Thoma liner eluded the Barons' outfielder. Much louder was the grand slam by a young Cuban American who had been all but unrecognizable to his teammates when he arrived for spring training in 1985 and who became inexorably tied to Huntsville lore. Until the team's demise, José Canseco and Mark McGwire—who never played together in Huntsville—were recalled as the signature players for the franchise, despite many other future All-Stars wearing a Huntsville uniform in the ensuing three decades. Between the two, Canseco and McGwire played fewer than 70 games at Joe Davis Stadium, but if everyone who claimed to have seen them actually did, the Stars would have set minor-league attendance records never to be matched.

With the massive multipurpose stadium—"The Joe" was also designed with high school football in mind, to help justify the construction—the Stars drew 300,810 in their inaugural season, an average of 4,178 per game. By 2014, as a lame-duck team already approved for transfer to Biloxi, the Stars were drawing a third of that figure.

It was suggested in a newspaper column in those dismal days that the best thing to happen to professional baseball in Huntsville would be for professional baseball to go away.

In the later years of the Miles Prentice ownership of the Stars, crowds were sparse at Joe Davis Stadium, 2013. *Courtesy Alabama Media Group.*

And…sure enough.

Here came the Rocket City Trash Pandas. Thousands jumped aboard the bandwagon, entranced by the nickname or just excited about baseball's return. Then the bandwagon got dragged to a halt by COVID-19. The April 15, 2020 opener was postponed, the stadium sitting empty and Trash Panda fans left only with the creativity of broadcaster Josh Caray, who, along with staffers Lucas Dolengowski and Nick Ceraso, aired a computer-simulated game against the Mississippi Braves, the would-be opponent. The Trash Pandas, for the record, won.

May 11, 2021, was the real deal. The Trash Pandas trotted out Lee Greenwood for the national anthem. More than 7,500 fans filled Toyota Field. For many, it was their first time in a large social setting in fifteen months. Reid Detmers, a No. 1 draft pick of the Angels, dazzled as the starting pitcher; by August, he was in the majors, one of ten Trash Pandas to be promoted to parent club Los Angeles Angels.

An hour or so before the opener, the Trash Pandas retired the No. 5 of Don Mincher. It was the inspiration of Ralph Nelson, the driving force to bring baseball to Madison but who had left his position as managing general partner and team president under a gray cloud only weeks earlier. The first

Reid Detmers was the starting pitcher in the Trash Pandas' first game. He then reached the majors by season's end in 2021. *Courtesy Rocket City Trash Pandas.*

World Series game Nelson ever saw in person featured a game-tying, ninth-inning single in Mincher's final major-league at bat. Mincher was a Lincoln Village kid, born when mill-league ball was thriving, then growing up as part of a thriving amateur program. During his major-league career, he made the All-Star team as an Angel first baseman. When he volunteered for a menial role with the fledgling Stars, he instead was offered the general manager's job. He put together a consortium of local owners to ensure the team would remain in Huntsville, becoming the team president. Ultimately, he became the president of the Southern League for nearly a dozen years.

Don Mincher did many great things in baseball. He did many things in baseball in a great way. Now resting at historic Maple Hill Cemetery, with a marker that reads "God, Family, Baseball," he is the thread that weaves through Huntsville's baseball history, from the mills to Madison, from feral shunks to Trash Pandas, to so many moments that, to someone with a baseball heart, felt nearly as grand and memorable as landing a man on the moon.

1

1903–1904

THE FIRST PRO TEAM AND THE FEUD WITH DECATUR

For more than a century, there has been a rivalry between Huntsville and Decatur, whether it's barbecue, culture or sports. It's white sauce and chicken on the Decatur side, red sauce and pork in Huntsville. Even as the cities evolved differently, there has been no shortage of civic pride, no suggestion that you'd find the two sides willing to sit around a campfire singing "Kumbaya."

Early in the twentieth century, thousands of acres of cotton fields separated the two cities. The Memphis & Charleston Railroad brought the most convenient transit, but travelers in their horse-drawn buggies could cross the Tennessee River by a ferry. Both ways provided a quicker access between the two cities than I-565 often does in current days.

When the cities became rivals in professional baseball, the *New Decatur Advertiser* assured its readers that "a club from (Huntsville) will fill the park to overflowing." Prescient words. Over the next two seasons, parks in both towns would fill with fans—and with controversy.

It was already the dog days of summer on August 1, 1903, when a group of representatives from four teams—Huntsville; what was then called the "Twin Cities" of Decatur and New Decatur; Columbia, Tennessee; and Pulaski, Tennessee—met to organize the Tennessee-Alabama State League. Reports from that meeting suggest "that the sport will soon be put upon a paying basis," thus leaving us with 1903 as something of the official debut of professional baseball in Huntsville. Certainly, previous "amateur" teams were paying some players, but the Tennessee-Alabama State League brought a modicum of organization to the process. J. Waddy Matthews, a scion of a prominent Huntsville family who would become a state bank examiner, was elected league president.

And when Huntsville came rolling into Decatur to open the season, "the-city-with-a-spring, sprung a surprise over us for two games and an endless number of home runs," according to the Decatur scribes. That launched Huntsville to a 22-7 season record, plenty to win the city's first pennant, as Decatur finished 15-15, Columbia 13-15 and Pulaski 9-21.

Even then, though, attendance was fickle. Manager W.M. Watkins wrote an open letter to fans to encourage larger crowds, saying the team wasn't supported as well as it should be. A portent of things to come.

The Huntsville-Decatur rivalry continued to simmer in 1904, after the Tennessee-Alabama State League expanded, bringing in Anniston, Bessemer, Chattanooga, Knoxville and Sheffield. Pulaski was jettisoned. The local media were all too happy to fan the flames of the Huntsville-Decatur feuds.

In a July editorial, the *Huntsville Daily Mercury* wrote of Decatur's "hoodlums and the rough element" that escalated the controversy. The owners, fans and players all seemed to despise one another. "Decatur is almost invariably wrong in everything," the *Mercury*'s baseball correspondent, whose name is sadly unrecorded, spat in disdain.

Suffice it to say, the Tennessee-Alabama League was not exactly the Swiss railroad system of minor-league operations to begin with. Then, when the July 4 holiday rolled around, it impulsively declared that a doubleheader scheduled for Decatur would instead be played at Huntsville's field. League rules permitted such a change, upon approval from both managers.

A crowd of 1,078—the largest of the season—watched from the grandstands and from their horse carriages for the bargain admission price of ten cents. The fans saw Huntsville sweep a doubleheader, leapfrogging ahead of Decatur in the standings, at 27-15 to 26-17, respectively.

That only served as kindling to controversy, with the real flames erupting later in the week, when Huntsville traveled to Decatur and feisty manager–third baseman Billy "Wee Wee" Prout was "attacked by a mob," according to the *Mercury*. Three Decatur citizens were later fined $7.50 for their roles in the brouhaha.

All this inspired what seemed equal parts consternation and whimsy in W.R. Van Valkenburgh, the president of Huntsville's baseball team, who wrote an open letter to Decatur mayor H.A. Skeggs, New Decatur mayor

Sam Blackwell and the sheriff of Morgan County. The *Mercury* was more than a little eager to offer the newsprint space:

> *DEAR SIR:*—*On next Thursday our baseball team is due to come to your city and play the Twin City team. Now, the last time down there, our team had some trouble. Of course, I don't know but one side of it and I don't pretend to say who was at fault in the matter, but I am told there were some fights. Now, we want to send our team back down there on next Thursday, provided, you and the sheriff can or will provide ample protection for the players and spectators so there will not be a repetition of it, and if anybody does start it, our players, our people and anybody else, have somebody there to arrest them and stop it.*

The baseball games' outcomes might be in doubt, but Mayor Skeggs won the war of words in a blowout.

> *DEAR SIR:*—*I have your favor of July 20th, and note what you say in reference to game to be played between Twin-City and Huntsville baseball teams next week. I thank you for calling my attention to the danger attendant upon the visit of the Huntsville baseball team to Decatur.*
>
> *The Twin-Cities, ordinarily, are as calm and peaceful as the placid bosom of the beautiful Tennessee on a June day; but when Huntsville comes to town with its baseball team, there is a danger of "something doing." The baseball park is situated outside of my jurisdiction, being in New Decatur. However, being mindful of the duties of every good citizen to maintain the majesty of the law under any and all circumstances, I agree with your suggestion that there ought to be sufficient force on the grounds when the Huntsville team and the Twin-City team contend for honors on the diamond, to maintain peace at any cost.*
>
> *With this in mind I have requested Governor Cunningham to send three regiments of state troops here to preserve order in this county and particularly at the ball park, on the days your team is to be here. If you think this force is not sufficient, I suggest that you have a peace warrant sworn out against the wild and wooly man from the West* [a reference to Prout] *who does stunts on the third base for Huntsville when he is not engaged in "awaiting" the Decatur umpire. Or if Huntsville courts do not believe that it is an offense against the law for the third baseman of the Huntsville team to "swat" the Decatur umpire and call him pet names that cannot be sent through the mail, then put him in a straight-jacket or amputate his strong*

right arm, all will be lovely and the goose will honk high. Or, if this will not do, muzzle him, and then if he succeeds in putting the umpire out of business, he will not be able to address him in the parliamentary language that is prevalent among ball players.

Van Valkenburgh began to insist on a neutral site but eventually accepted assurances there would be sufficient security. Huntsville agreed to send its team to Decatur. All would be lovely, the goose would apparently honk high and the *Mercury* pronounced a benediction on the whole mess: "It is hoped that no further trouble will occur and that the spirit of friendly rivalry between the two towns may be restored at the next meeting of the teams."

2

1911

AN ILL-FATED ENCORE AND THE FIRST GRADUATE
TO THE MAJORS

*J*ust as it became inevitable that any child christened Jordan during the latter part of the twentieth century would be tagged "Air," there was a similar laziness to nicknames one hundred years earlier, stealing from the already famous to apply a sobriquet to those sharing comparable names.

A diminutive outfielder of some renown in the nascent years of Major League Baseball was James "Ducky" Holmes, the result of a wiseacre's observation that the five-foot, seven-inch Holmes tended to waddle like a duck.

As Holmes's career begin to unfold, another James Holmes, thirteen years his junior, was growing up in the little burg of Lawrenceburg, Kentucky, home to a prosperous whiskey-maker whose products evolved into the famed Wild Turkey brand.

Jim Holmes resembled a duck in much the same way a pipe wrench resembles a calico cat. But he would inevitably become "Ducky" in the baseball world despite his long, lanky frame and the narrow oval face topped by dark hair parted crisply down the middle. He had a sly grin that suggested he was up to something, albeit a smile that witnessed the haphazard dental care of the day.

This "Ducky" Holmes goes into history as the first player from a Huntsville professional baseball team to "graduate" to the major leagues. A raw twenty-one-year-old, Holmes pitched for Huntsville's team in 1904 in the Tennessee-Alabama League, bedeviling the league with his tricky curveball.

Holmes lost his final appearance for Huntsville, a 3–2 decision at Chattanooga on August 19, the penultimate game of the season. Huntsville allowed two unearned runs, but the *Mercury* headline declared: "Umpire Was Rotten: And Chattanooga Won by a Single Run."

From Huntsville, Holmes moved from the Class C Augusta team directly to the Philadelphia Athletics. He made his major-league debut on September 8, 1906, for the Athletics against the New York Highlanders (later to become the Yankees) and pitcher "Happy Jack" Chesbro, who was a 41-game winner (yes, 41 wins!) in 1903. Holmes allowed a pair of runs in the second on a walk, a single and a triple but "gave great promise of becoming a crack pitcher" by retiring the next three, according to the *Philadelphia Inquirer*. Alas, he surrendered 6 more runs in the third, thanks to two errors and a hit batsman, in what the *Inquirer* labeled "one of the poorest played innings ever seen here."

Holmes pitched twice more for the Athletics that season then returned to Augusta for 1906 and 1907 before resurfacing with the Brooklyn Superbas in 1908 for a thirteen-game stint in his final major-league appearances.

That didn't end Holmes's pro career. He helped the Rochester Hustlers win three consecutive pennants in the minors and was such a popular figure among the Rochester faithful that they presented him with a diamond-studded wristwatch on the occasion of his being traded to rival Buffalo. The media adored him as well. There seemed to be a running joke with a Rochester sportswriter about Holmes's hitting skills, or lack thereof. Following a fluke 3-run double that won a game, the *Rochester Democrat and Chronicle* wrote, "Gray-haired fans say that Holmes, to their recollection, hasn't made a half dozen hits since Civil War days."

Holmes, a prankster at heart, got his revenge. One day, he trapped a rat during a road trip. He stuffed it inside a shirt box and dropped it in the middle of a table where teammates were playing cards. The rat later wound up, much like the horse's head in *The Godfather*, stuffed under the sheets of the sportswriter's hotel bed.

Holmes extended his pro career through the 1914 season. He found his way to Jacksonville, Florida, settling there with his wife and children, working as a grocer and occasionally helping out with Jacksonville's minor-league team until his death in 1960 at age seventy-seven.

The Huntsville season of 1904 was in turmoil from the get-go, with league officials bickering over the schedule less than a week into the season and juggling things to avoid extended and expensive road trips.

There was midseason tragedy when the wife of Huntsville outfielder Lawson Farris died on July 6 of septic fever only hours after delivering a child, who also soon died. Rivalry be damned, the Decatur team took up a collection and sent a wreath to be displayed at the grave site.

Coverage of the team in the *Mercury* was relatively consistent, but seldom was a player's first name included. Still, lack of in-depth reporting didn't mean there wasn't some entertainment: "Fierce and Rotten: Were the Umpire's Decisions in Sheffield Game." And there was this politically incorrect description of an injury-plagued team: "Cripples Beaten: The Huntsville Team Is in a Bad Shape."

Elsewhere in the league, a newspaper error irked a young Anniston Steelers outfielder. His name was printed as "Cyrus Cobb." It took little, as baseball historians know, to irk Tyrus Raymond Cobb.

Though Cobb's tenure in Anniston was brief, it has remained a revered part of that city's history. Civic leaders erected a plaque on the site of the boardinghouse where an eighteen-year-old Cobb lived in 1904, boldly if not accurately proclaiming him "the greatest baseball player of all time."

Cobb had flunked an audition for the Augusta Tourists, near his North Georgia hometown of Royston, but was encouraged to try out in Anniston. He left for Alabama with a warning from his strict father, a state senator who'd be brutally murdered by his wife the next year. "Don't come home a failure," he told his son.

Cobb found his game in Anniston. He hit well, and his hustle and grit were popular with fans. Stats weren't accurately recorded, but the website 78mag.com claims that Cobb batted .350. He was a robust self-promoter. He went to Scarborough Drug Store in downtown Anniston and scribbled out anonymous, glowing reviews, then mailed them to the Atlanta newspapers. Finally, they caught the attention of future sportswriting legend Grantland Rice, compelling Rice to make a trip to Anniston, after which he described Cobb as "a comet with a fiery tail."

The Anniston club folded in midseason, and Cobb was offered a second chance in Augusta. Then, by August 30, 1905, Cobb was in the majors with the Detroit Tigers, beginning a twenty-four-year career that has been the stuff of legend for more than a century.

So, if we can note that Jim Holmes was Huntsville's first major leaguer, we can also note that the first future Hall of Famer to play in a pro game in Huntsville was Ty Cobb.

COLONEL JOHN VAN VALKENBURG fit the unflattering description of "carpetbagger" as he settled in Huntsville following the Civil War. He had been wounded in battle and then a case of mistaken identity led to a dishonorable discharge from the Union army because a vengeful Indiana governor Oliver P. Morton believed him to be a critical newspaper editor by the same name. A cascade of support from his former troops cleared his name, but Van Valkenburg had been forever tarnished in his home state. He moved south, settling in Huntsville, working first as a planter, then opening a hardware business. Though he was a Yankee, the *Huntsville Weekly Democrat* was generous after his death in 1883: "He identified himself with the Southern people, by aiding in building up their material interests and ardently supporting Democratic men and measures....He was a kind and indulgent husband and father."

One of his five children was a son who'd own his mother's maiden name as his middle name. Wilfred Rodenbaugh Van Valkenburg joined his father in the hardware business and developed his own standing in the community as a civic leader.

W.R. Van Valkenburgh, who at some point attached the *h* to the end of his name, entered Huntsville royalty in 1883 at age twenty-one, marrying Emily Bradley, whose father owned the city's finest hotel and whose stepbrother was married to the daughter of Governor Thomas Bibb. The family moved into a home at 501 Franklin Street in 1902, a Queen Anne house that featured a stained-glass window depicting a scene from Homer's *Iliad*. It remains a gorgeous landmark in the Twickenham District, a reminder of a prosperous era in Huntsville when cotton was king.

In 1904, leaders from various Alabama communities began "taking active steps to organize baseball teams," according to a *Journal* report on March 10. W.R. Van Valkenburgh led the way and was elected president of the Huntsville Baseball Association, which pooled $1,500 in capital to form the team. Outfitted in dark blue uniforms with blue-and-white-striped socks, the Huntsville team opened play in May at West End Park, near where the Von Braun Center now stands.

Interest was so great that the team had an auxiliary ticket office at a downtown pharmacy. By midseason, even as the Decatur rivalry grew, there was league-wide resentment toward Huntsville. Van Valkenburgh was in full-tilt George Steinbrenner mode, it seemed. The Chattanooga newspaper reported that it was "a well-known fact that the Huntsville club [is] far out of the salary limit." Van Valkenburgh, it was claimed, said he'd have "a team to defeat Decatur if it cost $10,000 to get them together."

Perhaps it was Van Valkenburgh's largesse, or just the economic challenges of sports, but the Huntsville team began to mirror the financial difficulties across the Tennessee-Alabama State League.

In August, Van Valkenburgh and his board issued a public plea for support, writing in the *Mercury*, "We have worked hard to give the people of Huntsville some good sport and to be candid and frank with the public, will say, we have not been properly supported." With the exception of that controversial July 4 date with Decatur, the team lost money every day it played. They raised ticket prices for a late-August series with Decatur, but to no avail. An August 20 loss at Chattanooga, in which Huntsville managed only 2 hits, would be the last game.

Within a week, Van Valkenburgh posted this notice in the *Mercury*: "The Huntsville Baseball Assn. has decided to sell the fence, grand stand, bleachers, ticket office and all the wood work connected with the baseball park located now at West End.…We would like to sell this to the highest bidder, but we reserve the right to reject any and all bids."

Van Valkenburgh grew ill that fall. On March 21, only a few minutes after midnight, he died after what must have been a torturous illness. He was forty-three. With Van Valkenburgh's death, so died professional baseball in Huntsville—at least temporarily.

Mayor R.E. Smith proclaimed a "legal holiday" on May 11, 1911, between the hours of 3:00 p.m. and 6:00 p.m. Store proprietor Leo Marshuetz was offering two hundred free tickets to support the club. Baseball was back in Huntsville, sharing the headlines with the controversy over a "wet vs. dry" alcohol legalization issue. "Good men, keep your name off that whiskey petition," pleaded the *Daily Times*.

The Huntsville Westerns were competing in the Class D Southeastern League against the Anniston Models, Gadsden Steel Makers, Selma Centralites, Rome Hillies and Decatur Twins. It's not as if baseball had disappeared since 1904. The Huntsville Greys, a semipro team in the City League, won the title in 1908. But there was more cachet to having a professional team.

Huntsville and Decatur—of course—met in the season opener, with a trainload of Huntsville fans traveling west to root for their team. Fans unable to attend could gather at the Picto Theater on Washington Street at twenty-five cents a head to hear the game recreated by "an expert operator" from ticker-tape updates. Huntsville won, 7–3, in front of sixteen hundred fans, and the newspaper boldly predicted that "the Hunters with a little more effort can take the League pennant." Two days later, editorialists hopped on the bandwagon, writing, "We have already

Base Ball Suspends Business

Special to The Daily Times.

Decatur, Ala., May 6. – Mayor Skeggs, of Decatur and Mayor Patterson, of New Decatur, have issued a proclamation requesting the business men of their respective cities to close their places of business on next Monday, May 9, from 3 o'clock to 6 o'clock in the afternoon in order that the clerks and employes may be able to attend the game of baseball to be played between Decatur and Huntsville. It is said that the greater majority of the business houses at both cities will grant the request and close during the hours named.

This will be the opening game of the season of the Southeastern League and a large crowd is expected to attend the game. At least 1,000 are expected to be in attendance. At least 200 people are expected to attend from Huntsville.

Hunters 7; Decaturs 3; More Than 1600 Present

The local baseball fans who attended the opening of the baseball season in Decatur yesterday afternoon returned home last night much pleased with game, which resulted in a victory for the Hunters by a score of 7 as against Decatur's 3, which latter score was not made until the 8th. inning. It was a good game. The Hunters with a little more effort can take the League pennant. They started out well and it is predicted they will be able to take the game this afternoon and the one tomorrow. Thursday opens the season here with Decatur as the visiting team against the Hunters.

Left: So eager were cities for Opening Day that businesses were asked to shut down for the 1911 opener. *Huntsville Public Library*.

Right: The Hunters—the newspaper's nickname for the Huntsville team—knocked off Decatur in the 1911 season opener. *Huntsville Public Library*.

picked the Hunters as the winner of the league pennant." Then, after an 11–4 victory over Decatur in Huntsville's home opener, the paper offered "to make the game interesting…the Hunters in the future will have to keep the score down."

But so much for all the optimism. August headlines blared "Hoodoo Still Following the Hunters." Despite a midseason makeover in which new manager Arthur Riggs brought in twelve of his players from the Fort Smith, Arkansas team, Huntsville still finished 44-57, some 21 games behind first-place Anniston.

Among Riggs's players was twenty-year-old Charles Herbert "Chuck" Tompkins, a lean right-handed pitcher who became, after Jim Holmes, the second "graduate" to the big leagues from a Huntsville professional team.

In the pre-NCAA days, Tompkins sandwiched his season in Huntsville between playing college ball at Arkansas in 1911, then at Washington and Lee in 1912. The Cincinnati Reds signed him in 1912, prompting this report—complete with the extra *h* perhaps left over from a Van Valkenburgh typo—in the newspaper:

> *Charles Thompkins, a pitcher who recently joined the Cincinnati Reds, is a guileless youth, who looks like anything but a ball player. Some of the boys say he looks more like a Siberian crocodile, but there ain't no such animal. Mr. Thompkins, when he came to join the club, wandered*

for several hours before he located the hotel. When Hank O'Day wanted to know why he didn't ask a policeman, Mr. Thompkins explained that where he came from, nobody ever spoke to a policeman unless he wanted to surrender himself for some misdemeanor, and he, Mr. Thompkins, has not been misdemeaning any.

On Tuesday, June 25, 1918, the Reds were already trailing, 10–0, and fumbling their way to a seven-error game in the first half of a doubleheader in which Tompkins made his debut. He faced fourteen batters, allowing 5 hits, 1 run and striking out 1. He handled two fielding chances, making an error. He had 1 at bat, singling off future Hall of Famer Mordecai "Three-Finger" Brown.

It would be Tompkins's only major-league appearance. He'd finish his career as a 1.000 hitter and a .500 fielder.

Riggs, the journeyman who brought Tompkins to Huntsville, previously managed a whole collection of low-minor clubs, including the Camden Oauchitas, Argenta Shamrocks, Hot Springs Vaporites and Newport Pearl Diggers, before he transferred the nucleus of his Fort Smith team to Huntsville in May 1911.

He wasn't the type who wanted to establish permanent residence. Thirteen months later, Riggs was at it again. At that time, remember, Talladega was only slightly smaller than Huntsville. The hoopla and promise of spring 1911 had turned to rancor by the summer of 1912. At least one fan begged for some investigative journalism by the local scribes, to press the league panjandrums for some answers on the finances and the ease of the transfer to Talladega.

"Why," he pleaded, "was the franchise given up with no effort to sell it?… Why will they not give the fans and the small contributors some fact? Are they entitled to know?"

That might have necessitated pinning down Arthur Riggs, who, by the 1913 season, had moved on to Selma.

3

THE MILL TEAMS

BIGGER CROWDS THAN THE PROS

*T*he St. Louis Cardinals tried to woo Hub Myhand with a World Series ticket in 1928. He watched in awe as Babe Ruth hit three homers in one game as the Yankees swept St. Louis. Next, they sent him a train ticket, trying to lure him to spring training. But Myhand had pitched so long in the small southern towns of the low minors—Asheville to Bristol to Jackson to Tupelo—that the prospect of more bush-league cities and the disjointed lifestyle had no appeal.

Besides, he already had a good full-time job. He was the physical director for Dallas Manufacturing Company in Huntsville, a title and role that demonstrated the priority of athletics—baseball and basketball in particular—at the mills that were the heartbeat of Huntsville's economy.

It's not as if baseball disappeared in Huntsville following the demise of the pre–World War I pro teams. The sport was a fixture in the city well before and long after the pay-to-play guys moved along. There are records of teams and games in the late nineteenth century, often playing opponents from as far away as Cincinnati and luring hired talent that tiptoed on the boundaries of "amateur," "semipro" and "professional." The Monte Sano Hotel even had a team, the Katydids

The venues were unusual, too. They played indoor baseball at the Hippodrome, near Big Spring Park, and on June 3, 1908, the first night baseball game in the state of Alabama was played. A touring team of what was billed as "full-blooded Cherokee Indians" played an All-Star team from

THE HUNTSVILLE TIMES—HUNTSVILLE'S SESQUICENTENNIAL—SEPTEMBER 11-17, 1955

GREAT DALLAS TEAM OF 1931—Rated one of the best baseball teams ever produced in Huntsville is the 1931 Dallas baseball team pictured above. The team met and beat the best semi-pro teams in Alabama, Georgia and Tennessee. Members of the team, left to right, front row, Earl Allen; Woodrow Chisam, Norman Allen, Leslie Golden, Theron Fisher, Perry Chisam and Jim Tom Gentry. Back row, left to right, Rufus Crowson, H. E. (Hub) Myhand, Cowboy Fitch, Roy Green, John H. Tabor, Red Blount, Dick Adcock, Lawrence Hauer, Eugene Williams, Marvin Gentry, Pont Pinion, Dick Covington and Happy Koonce. The batboys are Ty Samples and Buddy Cobb. (Picture courtesy Hub Myhand)

Amateur teams like this one from Dallas Mill were more popular than the pros in the 1930s. *Huntsville Public Library.*

Huntsville's amateur league. The Indians traveled on a specially designed railcar that carried poles with fifty arc lights and a canvas fence that would be erected at the host field, in this case the fairgrounds park at West Clinton and Seminole. There were other distinguished visitors, too. Ty Cobb made a return visit in an exhibition game with the Detroit Tigers two decades after his unheralded visit as an Anniston Noble.

And there were even some undistinguished visitors, or so goes the saga passed down three generations. Lefty Williams, one of the disgraced players from the 1919 Black Sox scandal, was said to have pitched against one of Huntsville's semipro teams in the 1920s, albeit with the cloak of an assumed name.

The mills were the focal point for baseball from the late 1920s through the 1930s and were the foundation for a long, robust amateur baseball legacy. Thousands of fans would often show up for the intracity games, back when money was tight and other forms of entertainment were scarce. "The best entertainment in town—and most popular," wrote former *Times* sports editor John Pruett in a story for the Huntsville Historical Society. In what sounds implausible now, Huntsville's pro teams would occasionally play the mill teams on weekends when league schedules permitted, typically drawing the largest crowds the pros would entertain.

Though Huntsville was dubbed "The Water Cress Capital of the World," vast fields of cotton were the area's economic driver. With cheaper labor costs, companies began opening cotton mills across the South. Dallas Cotton Mills, named for a Nashville textile industrialist, was opened in Huntsville in 1891 at a cost of more than $1 million. That began the boom that birthed the slogan "Happy, Hustling Huntsville." Soon to follow were Merrimack, Madison Spinning Mill, Margaret Mill and West Huntsville Cotton Mills. The latter was founded by a former resident of Pierre, South Dakota, Tracy Pratt, soon to become a fixture as a civic leader. At his passing in 1928, the *Daily Times* proclaimed, "It is generally agreed that he was responsible for more of the major industries locating in Huntsville than any man who ever resided here, and was Huntsville's First Citizen."

But it was H.E. "Hub" Myhand who was Huntsville's First Citizen of Baseball.

His arrival coincided with the construction of Dallas Park, not far from the mill villages and what still stands as a monument to those days, now known as Optimist Park. "Merrimack would bring in a lot of good players for the summer and give them jobs—college boys who were outstanding players," Myhand said in a 1979 interview.

> *Lincoln did the same thing. At Dallas, we used mostly home-grown boys and we usually did all right.*
>
> *All of the teams were pretty even and the competition was pretty lively. I never did see it get out of hand, but we had some pretty good scraps. And everybody in town seemed to be pretty involved in it. I can remember when there was a Class D team in Huntsville…and if they were playing a game on the same day as the mill teams, they didn't have anybody in the stands. Everybody was out watching the mill teams.*

The Lincoln and Dallas teams merged in 1935, effectively ending the mill-team rivalries, and numerous labor problems plagued the mills, which began placing less emphasis on athletics. As Myhand began focusing on youth sports, there was a willing successor to his "Mr. Baseball" role—and a new avenue for fans and players.

An ex-navy man named Jim Talley was arguably the city's top amateur player in the post–World War II years, and he began organizing top talent to surround him. The Huntsville Boosters, in 1950, became the city's first team to reach the National Baseball Congress World Series in Wichita, Kansas. That soon became a habit for Huntsville teams. A strong local independent league blossomed, producing generations of talent, from Don Mincher in the 1950s to Dave Beck and Ricky and Randy Davidson. There was also the shortstop who turned down a $100,000 signing bonus from the Montreal Expos to become the University of Tennessee's first Black quarterback, a young man named Condredge Holloway, still acclaimed as the best athlete in city history.

"Back before people had TVs and boats and cars and before drive-ins, going to the baseball game was the thing to do," Talley told John Pruett in 1979. "That's why we had the big crowds, and why there were so many good players around here. We had good baseball players 15 cents a dozen. Now, for what they pay ballplayers, you could've filled forty teams.

"I believe," Talley said, "those were what we called 'the good old days.'"

4

THE 1930s

THE "PEPPY" SPRINGERS CAN'T SURVIVE

*W*all Street had crashed, but the ripples had yet to hit Huntsville in 1930. In fact, the city celebrated the grand opening of the posh Hotel Russel Erskine on Friday, January 3. More than 4,000 residents—from a population of 10,500, according to the recent census—toured the modern building and viewed "the tastefully designed and skillfully decorated interior." The namesake was a Huntsville native who had gone on to become president of the Studebaker Company. (Alas, the Depression ultimately took its toll on the automotive industry, and a nearly broke Erskine committed suicide in 1933, taking responsibility for Studebaker's financial crisis.)

Six weeks later, a small blurb appeared in the newspaper. Representatives from the Class D Georgia Alabama League were visiting Huntsville to discuss having a team here. That very week, the town was rocked by the unexpected deaths of two former mayors. Dr. John D. Humphrey died of a heart attack at age seventy-nine—"a mighty oak has fallen," proclaimed the *Daily Times*. The next day, R.E. "Earl" Smith was struck by a car and succumbed two days later. (Smith's term in office was highlighted by a street fight with newspaper editor J. Emory Pierce in 1912, after which the chagrined mayor fined himself ten dollars.)

Two days later, a happier banner headline appeared across the top of page one: "Baseball Franchise Comes Here."

League president L.H. Carre, an Anniston resident, made the announcement that the former Gadsden franchise would be transferred to

The return of professional baseball was enormous news for Huntsville readers in 1930. *Huntsville Public Library.*

Huntsville, joining a league that included Anniston and Talladega as other Alabama teams and Carrollton, Cedartown and Lindale in Georgia.

The move was easier reported than done. There was a substantial challenge in funding. Local leaders made a pitch to their neighbors to pony up support, with a tactic that rang as true then as now. The economic impact from dollars spent would be significant, and the publicity throughout the South from stories about the team would have intangible benefits. Spearheaded by city council president James Gill and W.T. Hutchens, a former mayor, long-term postmaster and former mill-league baseball player, the effort cobbled together enough money to make the team a reality. A 2,500-seat park was planned, and Bill Pierre, a journeyman minor-league catcher, was hired as manager.

Some thirty-five to forty aspirants auditioned for Pierre. "A peppy lot," offered the *Daily Times*, adding that "it has been a long time since (Pierre) has seen an aggregation of players who are keenly interested in a ball club as these players are." So promising was this team that Joe "Squatty" Amadee, author of a pair of no-hitters the previous season, wouldn't last the season. Thus fans were deprived of the occasion to have Squatty removed from a game by Tubby—Pierre's managerial successor, W.H. "Tubby" Walton.

Some things don't change. Even then, there was a public contest to come up with a nickname. But only suggestions from women were considered. A committee chose Springers, which had been entered by

Mrs. Harold "Margaret" Herrin and Miss Mary Hauer, both of whom were awarded season tickets. Team ownership seemed to take extraordinary measures to entice female fans, and local proprietors joined in the effort. Ladies buying a dress at Sam Schiffman's ("The Friendly Store") on Thursday before the opening game received a season ticket. The first ten women who spent five dollars or more at Dunnavant's on the same day were given a season ticket. Simply stopping into Gross-Stockton Chevrolet would earn a season ticket, and slightly less glamorously, the first ten ladies who ordered a ton or more of coal or coke from Latham Cole & Coke got the ticket bonus.

There was unabashed optimism in the community for the Springers, despite some losses to the amateurs on the local mill teams and the 14–2 drubbing at Cedartown on May 8 in the season opener. The excitement over the home debut was contagious, and with no shortage of pageantry. Local banker Ashford Todd was announced as the first official ticket buyer. Spring Branch Park was looking spiffy, with four-seat boxes available for twenty-five dollars for the season. And, in sobering reality of the time, it was noted that a grandstand was built on the right side for "colored fans."

Huntsville set its sights on the league's attendance trophy, which would require three thousand for the opener. Stores were closing early on May 9 for the game, and a parade would begin at 2:00 p.m. Mayor Aleck W. McAllister was going to throw out the first pitch, with Dillard catching it. Local merchants offered prizes to players, like three pairs of silk underwear to the first Springer to reach base safely.

SPRINGERS WIN FROM ANNISTON IN GREAT GAME

Hig Gets Five Hits and Four Runs During Game

CROWDER STRIKES OUT ELEVEN MEN

President of League Is Official Visitor Here Wednesday Afternoon

Everything was right for the Springers yesterday afternoon, the local club playing better ball than on any former occasion since its organization, and every man doing his part for victory. The play was so good, the hits so timely, and the pitching of Crowder so exceptional that the visiting Anniston Nobles fell by the way side by a nine to three score.

Higginbotham was hot yesterday. He got two homers, hit for two bases and clouted two singles, scoring a total of three men by his batting. In addition he had three chances in the field and made all of them good.

Wolfe, clever shortstop, took some awful chances and yet missed two easy ones. However he connected with the old apple in the early part of the game for three bases. Two baggers were hit by Hammond, Patterson and McSwain for the local club, while McGee who plays first base for Anniston jumped two two baggers in the rough. He also scored once. Fugua, Anniston shortstop, connected for three bags and also scored once. The third Anniston run was made by Goode, the Noble shortstop.

Lefty Crowder pitched masterful baseball, retiring eleven of the visitors by the strikeout route. The first three men facing him went down swinging. Though he showed a tendency toward wildness at times and walked four men, he nevertheless managed to strikeout eight more men during the contest.

L. H. Carre, of Anniston, president of the Georgia-Alabama League and L. M. Carre, secretary of the league were here as distinguished visitors to the game yesterday, having some official business in connection with the club.

Tubby Walton and Earnest Thompson both made thei rinitial appearances here as the new pilots of the club. Each made a great impression on the local fans who wish them well.

The play by play record and box score follows:

First Inning

Anniston: Goode strikes out. Dixon strikes out. Walker strikes out

For a while, everything was bright and shiny for Huntsville baseball in 1930. *Huntsville Public Library.*

The Springers clobbered Cedartown, 9–1, and an instant hero was crowned in right fielder Clarence Higginbotham, who homered twice. Higginbotham would hit more than 20 homers and bat over .340 for the season but was sold late in the season to Anniston, much to the chagrin of local fans.

Soon, reality sank in for the pro baseball franchise that could look across town and find it not the least bit unusual to see crowds of 3,500 watching the local lads of Dallas Mill play Merrimack. Truth be told, the most excitement and biggest crowds for the Springers occurred on those weekends when they took a break from the Georgia-Alabama League schedule to play exhibitions against the mill teams.

Within ten days of the opener, there was this headline: "Disappointed in Huntsville: Small Attendance and Support of Baseball Here Is Discouraging."

"The players themselves are disheartened and the backers of the baseball are disgusted in a measure," wrote the *Daily Times*. It reported that less than eighty dollars was collected at the gate each game. At the midpoint of the season, the newspaper made an unabashed plea for the "moral support" of the players and continuing publicity for the city. The roster underwent wholesale changes, there were rumors of a potential sale to Atlanta investors and ultimately five managers tried to lead the team.

The Springers limped to the finish with a 35-66 record, worst in the league. Their final day was a debacle, losing a doubleheader to Cedartown, 11–8 and 15–6. So miserable was the performance that manager Clarence Hart fined one player, Hammond, twenty-five dollars for loafing.

With a rare bylined story, under the suspicious nom de plume "Peter Piper," the *Daily Times* was viciously critical after the double loss. "Cedartown would have a much harder time against the *Daily Times* carrier boys." And, "Let's hope the management will be able to live down the disgrace during the cold winter months."

The cold winter brought an end to the Georgia-Alabama League. There would be no more professional baseball in Huntsville for another half century.

5
1985

THE STARS SHINE

*J*osé Canseco reported to spring training in February 1985 listed at six feet, three inches and 185 pounds, the measurements from the previous season. Bruce Robinson, a former A's catcher and special instructor who worked with Canseco at Class A Modesto in August 1984, recalled that Canseco had ballooned so much "I didn't even recognize him."

Playing for essentially the junior varsity with roster hopefuls and reserves, Canseco homered in the Athletics' first intrasquad game of spring training. He hit such blasts that A's manager Jackie Moore quipped, "We might have to put a cop on Van Buren Road [outside the stadium] to direct traffic when he takes batting practice." Canseco, the *San Francisco Examiner* dutifully reported, "does weight training to isolate specific power muscles."

Ultimately, we learned he was doing weight training with a little juice on top. Heretofore, baseball's brush with the world of pharmaceuticals had been either illegal or unspoken. Players had long taken "greenies," amphetamines that some could claim were little more than what a couple cups of strong coffee might provide in caffeine content. More devastating, federal investigators in 1985 were furiously working on a case that saw more than a dozen players brought to trial and punished for their cocaine use. Many others were linked to the drug, including stars like Dave Parker, Keith Hernandez and Tim Raines, and a sourpuss outfielder who'd become the Huntsville Stars' manager in 1998, Jeffrey Leonard.

Canseco proudly acknowledged his use of steroids, even calling his autobiography *Juiced*. He referred to himself as a "modern-day Frankenstein." He unabashedly talked about performance-enhancing drugs, alleged that 85

Left: Though José Canseco's homers never cleared the highway, it didn't keep fans from calling him José Parkway. *Johnny Phillips collection*.

Right: José Canseco, 1985. *Courtesy Alabama Media Group*.

percent of major leaguers were on PEDs and that he and teammate Mark McGwire injected each other in the buttocks with PEDs. A Huntsville gym owner admitted in an interview with John Pruett of the *Huntsville Times* that he procured steroids for Canseco.

The Huntsville franchise had for decades an uncomfortable tie to performance-enhancing drug use. Four ex-Stars—Canseco, Jason Giambi, Miguel Tejada and Ryan Braun—were named Most Valuable Players in the majors and all were linked to PEDs. McGwire's chase of Roger Maris's record became tainted when his use was reported by the Associated Press. Slugger Nelson Cruz was suspended for 50 games for steroid use. It even filtered into the Stars' clubhouse, where only the most naive observer would have believed that some of the Stars' massive bodies were, well, the result of training of specific power muscles.

(One ex-Star gained notoriety for being a stickler for rules. Pitcher Mike Fiers revealed the Houston Astros' sign-stealing system in a November 2019 story in *The Athletic*. Fiers pitched for the Stars in 2010 and 2011, going 6-4 with 6 saves working as both a reliever and a starter. He threw eight innings of 3-hit ball at Chattanooga in his final game for the Stars.)

Canseco's numbers in Huntsville were as inflated as his biceps. After only 47 homers in his first 372 minor-league games, he belted 25 home runs in 58 games for the Stars, then added 11 more after a call-up to Class AAA and 5 while playing part-time for Oakland in the latter part of 1985. As the American League Rookie of the Year in 1986, he had 33 homers in 600 at bats, including 2 off Roger Clemens, another star linked to steroids.

Canseco also hit for average—.318 at Huntsville; his OPS, before the stat was popularized, was 1.146—and had good defensive skills, something that faded late in his career. Despite playing just half of a season in Huntsville, his 25 homers and 80 RBIs earned him the league's Most Valuable Player honors. (That would be 62 homers and 199 RBIs over the course of a 144-game schedule.) As he later wrote, "I set so many records it was a joke."

He was the city's first superstar, and citizens remained worshipful as he became a major-league sensation. Canseco built friendships in Huntsville, whether with fans, batboys or strangers he met at local restaurants. Alas, as the years left him cash-strapped and his reputation tarnished, he refused an invitation to return to Huntsville during the Stars' final season unless the club provided first-class airfare.

INCUMBENT MAYOR JOE W. Davis was launching his reelection campaign in 1984 when he was approached with a proposal by an ex-coach named Larry Schmittou: Build me a ballpark, and I'll bring you a minor-league team.

Schmittou was an ultra-successful baseball coach at Vanderbilt University and had been recruiting coordinator for the football team before the NCAA added another rule to its encyclopedia of regulations, prohibiting coaches from "double-dipping" in multiple sports. When he lost the football gig at Vandy, he also lost a big chunk of salary. A gregarious personality and promoter, Schmittou decided to take his talents to minor-league baseball.

Along with the affable Farrell Owens, he built Herschel Greer Stadium and brought the Sounds' Class AA Southern League team to Nashville. His empire grew to other cities. Eventually, Triple A wanted to be in a thriving market like Nashville, but what would Schmittou do with his Sounds?

In August 1984, he began negotiating with Huntsville, but time was of the essence. Council member Jane Mabry, a feisty mother of three and former French horn player in the University of Alabama band, slowed the process during council meetings. She called Schmittou's sales pitch of dazzling numbers about attendance and economic impact and tax revenue "pie in the sky."

Then there was the beer issue. Huntsville was considerably more conservative in those days, and Mabry was a contrarian there, too. During a council work session, she asked what would happen if beer sales weren't permitted. Schmittou flatly responded, "Then I don't come."

Seeing the potential team slipping away because of his political opponent's obstinance, Joe Davis went into compromise mode. He asked Schmittou to make half of the stadium drinking, the other half nondrinking. Finally, Schmittou agreed to establish no-alcohol sections, and Davis continued to plead with the council. Finally, in a formal vote, it was approved, four to one—Mabry in dissent—for the city to pay for the stadium out of the general operating budget.

One of the "yea" votes came from a young restaurateur named Tommy Battle, who grew up in Birmingham and who would serve only a single term on the council. His future job as Huntsville mayor in the 2010s would frustratingly coincide with a failed and distant team ownership led by Miles Prentice, and then he'd watch with interest as a political foe, a developer named Louis Breland, provided the land for a new stadium in neighboring Madison. (Nonetheless, even though representing Huntsville, Battle eagerly packed Rocket City Trash Pandas merchandise to distribute to his hosts on a business development / goodwill visit to Japan in 2019.)

In the spirit of cooperation, Schmittou promised he'd expand the no-alcohol area from one section of seats to a larger area if the demand rose. When the Stars left Joe Davis Stadium in 2014, it was still just one section.

For years, Schmittou took great delight in teasing Don Mincher, the general manager of the Stars in 1985. You already have the hype of a debut season, so you don't also need to win the pennant *and* have a transcendent player. It's overkill. "This is the worst thing that can happen to Huntsville. You don't need to have the best team you ever had the first year," Schmittou said.

The lineup that manager Brad Fischer rolled out on opening night had a number of future major leaguers.

CF Luis Polonia	2B Brian Graham
C Charlie O'Brien	3B Ray Thoma
LF Stan Javier	DH Rocky Coyle
RF José Canseco	SS John Marquardt
1B Rob Nelson	P Tim Belcher

It was O'Brien who hit the first homer to travel outside the park in the 10–0 romp over Birmingham, and he became the first Star to be promoted

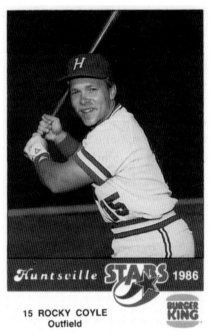

Left: Brad Fischer was the Stars' first manager in 1985. *Johnny Phillips collection.*

Right: Rocky Coyle was the most popular player among fans on the early Stars teams. *Johnny Phillips collection.*

to the majors, for a June 2 debut. All told, fifteen players from that club eventually reached the big leagues.

The Stars were second in the Southern League in homers, batting average and runs. "They put on a show every night," said Bob Mayes, who covered the Stars for the *Huntsville Times*. They finished 78-66, only the fourth-best record among the teams, but won the first-half Western Division pennant on Canseco's coattails. That sent them to the playoffs in September, where they knocked off Knoxville, 3 games to 1, and into the championship against Charlotte.

The Stars clobbered the O's, 11–0, in the opener, scoring 3 two-out runs in the third. They made it two in a row when Brian Dorsett hit an 0-2 pitch for a walk-off single. Back in Charlotte, the O's won game three, helped along by a homer from Tom Dodd, who has made his post-baseball home in Decatur. Then came a 9-run Huntsville second inning in the fourth game, only to have Charlotte chisel away and take an 11–10 victory. Said pitcher

John Habyan to Charlotte writer Stan Olson, "You sure can't see anything like this on cable."

The same could almost describe the drama in the decisive game on September 13. Pete Kendrick, who once threw a phenomenal 257 pitches to win both games of a WAC Tournament doubleheader for Brigham Young, was the Huntsville starter. His slow curve frustrated the O's, who found themselves down 2–0 after the first on a Nelson single and infield out. However, Charlotte tagged Kendrick in a 3-run fifth before Mike Ashman's double tied the game in the eighth.

Up came Rocky Coyle in the ninth. He hit the second pitch he saw from Mark Leiter for a homer to center and a 4–3 lead. The Stars tacked on another run, then set down the O's in order in the ninth and began to celebrate the first pro baseball championship in Huntsville since 1903.

Coyle retired following the 1987 season, after a short stay in the Toronto organization, moving to North Carolina. He has worked as a youth minister, pastor and coach since his retirement. He still maintains many friendships in Huntsville, and for all of Canseco's power, Coyle was remembered more sentimentally by loyal longtime Stars fans. Indeed, when a Stars booster club created an annual award to the player who exemplified hustle, team spirit and determination, it was a simple choice. They named the award "The Rocky."

6

THE OAKLAND A's ERA

SOME MEMORABLE NAMES, INCLUDING A VISITING SHOOTING GUARD

*W*ho could have imagined that a year later Huntsville fans would have a second player for whom they would wax nostalgically and wistfully decades later? Though, it must be noted, the recollections were pretty much one-sided. "I really don't remember much about Huntsville," Mark McGwire confessed to an inquiring reporter one evening in the early 2000s.

As a third baseman, McGwire seldom drew comparisons to Brooks Robinson. He had been a star at Southern Cal and a member of the U.S. team in the 1984 Olympics, before baseball was officially a medal sport for the Olympic Games. He had been drafted as a pitcher by Montreal but chose college ball, and the Trojans employed him at first base and third. (A USC teammate frequently in search of the strike zone was a lefty named Randy Johnson.) McGwire played 55 games for Huntsville, batting .303 with 10 homers and 53 RBIs. The Stars repeated as Western Division champs in 1986, again winning 78 games in the regular season. But after eliminating Knoxville, they came up a win short in the championship series to Columbus. Terry Steinbach was the catcher and Walt Weiss was at shortstop. Coyle had a pair of homers in a key postseason game, further cementing his legacy. Greg Cadaret and Kirk McDonald both finished 12-5.

Canseco was in the majors in '86, en route to the American League Rookie of the Year award. The next season, the honor went to McGwire, then to Weiss; Oakland is the only AL team to have three consecutive winners.

Huntsville hosted the Southern League All-Star Game in 1986, and Steinbach—later selected the league's MVP—was the game's MVP. Two

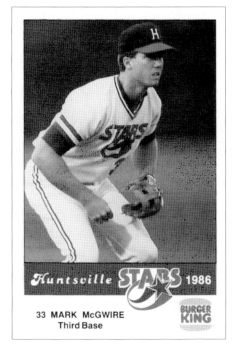 

Left: Mark McGwire was a third baseman and only beginning to show signs of power with Huntsville. *Johnny Phillips collection*.

Right: Terry Steinbach was an All-Star MVP at two levels. *Johnny Phillips collection*.

years later, he was the Major League All-Star Game MVP after homering off Dwight Gooden in his first All-Star Game at bat and delivering the American League's only other run on a sacrifice fly. Steinbach had homered in his first at bat as a big leaguer, and All-Star teammates were telling him he was "an answer to a trivia question."

Only a few days before that Southern League All-Star Game, a young outfielder named Vincent "Bo" Jackson sped into the Memphis Chicks' parking lot in his Alfa Romeo, running late because he'd lost his hotel key. It was June 30, and this marked his Southern League debut as a Kansas City Royals' farmhand. Jackson was fresh from his Heisman Trophy–winning season at Auburn but opted for baseball after turning down an offer from the penurious Hugh Culverhouse, the owner of the Tampa Bay Buccaneers, who'd made him the top pick in the NFL draft. Bo drew massive crowds across the Southern League in his brief tenure, particularly in his native Birmingham and in Huntsville. One of his games in Huntsville was even broadcast live on local television.

In his debut, Jackson was 1-for-4 with an RBI grounder up the middle in his first at bat. A reporter asked him after the game if he retrieved the ball from his first hit. Jackson smugly said, "My trophy case is already full."

IN 1987, BRAD FISCHER was in his third and final season as the Stars' manager and didn't find his lineup quite as loaded as in 1985. Though they won the second half, they were quickly kayoed in the division finals by Birmingham. The bottom fell out in 1988, even with Canseco briefly in the lineup. That would be twin brother Ozzie, who managed only a .222 average with 3 homers and 12 RBIs in 27 games, striking out in 1 of every 3 at bats.

While the A's reached three consecutive World Series, from 1988 through 1990, they were a small-market team. One could make the argument that keeping the big-league train running siphoned resources from the minors. The Stars won the second half in 1989 and were eliminated in the first round, then had the division's best overall record in 1990 but failed to win either half and sat out the playoffs. With each passing year, the list of impactful graduates into the majors dwindled. Then there was Todd Van Poppel.

Van Poppel, a six-foot, five-inch Texan with a blazing fastball, dominated his high school opponents. He was atop most of the teams' draft charts in the spring of 1990. But he warned the Braves, who had the No. 1 pick, not to waste it on him, that he was going to the University of Texas.

The Braves passed, and so did the next dozen teams. Oakland GM Sandy Alderson took a chance. He drafted Van Poppel, who ultimately agreed to sign for a $500,000 bonus. He made eight starts in A ball before being assigned to Huntsville in 1991. There he went 6-13 with 90 walks in 132 innings, and the A's promoted him for a cameo start in September at the ripe age of nineteen. Sadly, he became the poster child for a pitcher being brought up too quickly, pitching his last game as a thirty-two-year-old with a 40-52 career record and an ERA of 5.58.

So, for the Atlanta Braves, what to do with that No. 1 draft pick Van Poppel

Todd Van Poppel was a controversial first-round draft pick. *Johnny Phillips collection.*

cautioned them not to spend? They had their eye on a shortstop at the Bolles School in Jacksonville, a kid named Larry Wayne Jones, whom family and friends called Chipper.

The 1992 Stars made the playoffs and enjoyed the first no-hitter in franchise history, a combined effort by Dana Allison, Roger Smithberg and Todd Revenig. But they were eliminated by Chattanooga, which was then steamrolled by a Greenville team that included Javy Lopez, Chipper Jones and Eddie Perez and is arguably the best in league history.

If you've somehow gone through life without hearing of Quinsigamond Community College, a two-year school in Worcester, Massachusetts, you're not alone. Twenty-two rounds after taking the flyer on Van Poppel, the A's selected the Quinsigamond third baseman, a local kid named Tanyon Sturtze. But scout J.P. Ricciardi, a future major-league general manager and "Moneyball" disciple, visited Sturtze and told him the A's planned to transform him into a pitcher.

It worked, though not without growing pains. Sturtze was 5-12 in 1993, but one of those wins was the team's first solo no-hitter. He won 6 games the following year before the Cubs scooped him up in the Rule 5 draft. He went on to pitch twelve seasons in the majors and was briefly a key member of the Yankees bullpen. It was on the occasion of his return to Massachusetts in a Yankees uniform that his mother, Linda, told the *New York Times*: "Wherever he goes, we support him, whether he's a Yankee or anywhere else. Of course, I get a lot of comments from people like, 'Why isn't he a Red Sox?' I say, 'Because the Yankees are paying him, that's why.'"

THE STARS WENT THROUGH a stretch with only one playoff appearance—and a single meager win—in four seasons, and things also got dicey off the field. In 1993, Schmittou began considering selling or moving the team. There were eager marketplaces—it seemed for a while the Southern League would even wind up with a franchise in San Juan, Puerto Rico—and Schmittou was putting more of his focus on his Triple A clubs. In November 1993, a group led by Don Mincher provided Schmittou with a letter of intent to buy the club. But negotiations during the winter were tumultuous. It was not until April 13, 1994—less than twenty-four hours before the season opener—that the final paperwork was signed, securing the team's future in Huntsville. The consortium of owners included Mincher; local businessman Donn Jennings; local physicians Richard Harris, Ray Shepard, Calame Sammons and Michael Caruso; investment banker Phil Dotts; accountants Ed Rowe and

Arthur Faulkner; attorney Joe Ritch; financial consultant Wayne Gregory; country music star Randy Owen from the group Alabama; and Fort Payne businessman Brant Craig, a longtime friend of Owen.

Huntsville won its second pennant in 1994 with few brand-name players on board. Nonetheless, it won 81 games for the best winning percentage in franchise history, proof that prospects don't always equate to winning. Gary Jones, a Stars second baseman only eight years earlier, did a superb managing job. Jason Giambi played 56 games and hit an anemic .223 with only 6 homers. John Wasdin, on the eve of a twelve-year journeyman career in the majors, won 12 games to lead a pitching staff that carried an uninspiring offense.

As a strike paralyzed Major League Baseball, the Stars went to Zebulon, North Carolina, and split the first two playoff games, with an Ernie Young homer boosting Wasdin to a win in the second game. Returning to Huntsville, the Stars won the next two, with Jason Wood driving in 4 runs with 1 homer and 2 doubles.

Wood, the Southern League MVP, is a baseball lifer. He played in 1,890 minor-league games and had 1,840 hits. He also had some brief appearances in the show with Oakland, Detroit and the Marlins. In a long coaching career, he was most recently the coordinator of infield instruction for the Giants. Young, too, has enjoyed a long career in the game. He won an Olympic gold medal with Team USA in 1990, played parts of eight seasons in the majors, coached and managed in the minors, then went full circle in 2021 by serving as a Team USA coach in the Tokyo Olympics.

However, Jason Wood, Ernie Young, the Stars' pennant and the MLB strike were mere footnotes to the 1994 Southern League season, when the spotlight was stolen by a .202 hitter for the Birmingham Barons.

Bo Jackson had his Alfa Romeo. Michael Jordan had his bus, which, contrary to popular belief, he did not purchase. The Barons simply leased the bus—at last report, it was still running charters to Mississippi casinos for an undisclosed owner—because it was a little more luxurious and spacious than others, and with more security elements.

Jordan started out 0-for-8, then sighed that his first hit was "a little better [than his first NBA basket]. When I started basketball, everybody knew I would get at least two points."

A signature moment for him came on April 28, 1994, in Huntsville, where a crowd of 11,034 saw Jordan hit a two-out, 2-run double that gave the Barons a win over the Stars. Video from the game shows a lanky hitter with a slight hitch in his swing and a very tall strike zone. On the bases, he ate

A weak-hitting Barons outfielder named Michael Jordan packed 'em into the stands throughout the Southern League. *Courtesy Alabama Media Group.*

up the ground with incredibly long strides, making up for extremely poor fundamentals. You know the rest of the story. The itch to return to basketball was too much, and Jordan was back in the NBA the following March.

THOUGH 1995 AND 1996 brought Huntsville's only consecutive losing seasons to that point, and with few names that stood out on the marquee, the 1997 Stars were the best offensive team in franchise history. They scored a league-record 942 runs, bashing 164 homers, with a .268 team batting average. One night in July, they annihilated Chattanooga, 22–3, with 7 homers, 23 hits and 47 total bases. They were never shut out, but, conversely, only shut out an opponent once. Pitcher Steve Connelly, who made his post-baseball home in Huntsville, laughed, "From what I remember, as a pitching staff we needed that many runs."

Nineteen of forty-two players eventually reached the majors, including outfielder Ben Grieve, the Southern League MVP with a .328/24/108 line in 100 games. Mike Neill had a league-record 129 runs scored and hit .340. Mike Coolbaugh, whose life would shockingly end when he was struck by a line drive while coaching first base for Tulsa in 2007, led the league with 30 homers and 132 RBIs. Miguel Tejada, the future AL MVP, was at shortstop, and though he could often make routine plays look adventurous, he handled tricky hops like a magician and drove home 97 runs with 22 homers.

The team's storybook moment was written by a player who wasn't there during the regular season. Justin Bowles ended his year at Class A and flew home to Houston. But the Stars had a roster vacancy, and Bowles was ordered to Mobile to join the Stars on the road.

He missed his flight—and the playoff opener—when he was stuck in traffic at a railroad crossing. He idled on the bench until the ninth inning of the fourth game. With two runners on, two out, the Stars trailing 2-1

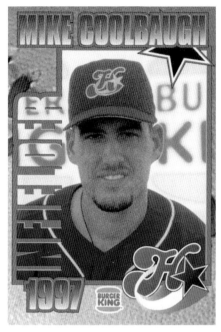

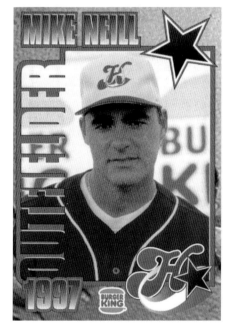

Above, left: Mike Coolbaugh tragically died when he was struck by a foul ball while coaching at Arkansas. *Johnny Phillips collection.*

Above, right: Shortstop Miguel Tejada became the AL MVP in 2002. *Johnny Phillips collection.*

Left: Mike Neill, a big bopper on the 1997 team, also won gold for Team USA in the Sydney Olympics. *Johnny Phillips collection.*

in the series and 5–2 in the game, manager Mike Quade called on Bowles to pinch-hit. On a 3-2 pitch, he channeled Rocky Coyle. He homered to tie the game. Neill's walk-off homer in the tenth sent the Stars to Game 5, where a 7-run first inning all but clinched the West title. Alas, there was no magic left. The depleted Stars lost to Greenville in 5 games of the championship series, leaving Neill to bemoan, "If we'd won this thing, we'd have gone down as one of the best teams in league history, but now we're just another team."

Justin Bowles became a starting outfielder for Huntsville in 1998. He was joined most nights by Roberto Vaz, a former University of Alabama hero who would make his home in Huntsville, and Mario Encarnación, a preternaturally talented Dominican Republic native who was found dead in 2005 in Taiwan in the dormitory for the Chinese team for which he was playing. The transportation for his body and his headstone were paid for by Miguel Tejada, his Huntsville teammate and lifelong friend.

Those Stars also featured Eric Chavez, a raw third baseman who made 14 errors in 79 games for a .935 fielding percentage but spent constant pregame hours working on his defense. Only three times in sixteen major-league seasons did he make that many, each time during a full season of play. He had a career fielding average of .970 at third, winning six Gold Gloves.

Tim Hudson, embraced in Huntsville as a former Auburn All-SEC pitcher, won 10 games and had a 4.54 ERA but was still honing his control. Hudson went on to win 222 games with the A's, Braves and Giants, then returned to his beloved Auburn as an assistant coach.

But you could feel the tension building between the Oakland parent club and the Stars. No one was more acutely aware of player-development priorities than an ex–big leaguer like Don Mincher, but while 1997 was the source of great entertainment, there was something about it that left a sour taste for the team president. The Athletics made many late-season promotions, decimating the playoff-bound Stars. The following season, the A's assigned the ornery Jeffrey "Hac-Man" Leonard as the manager, a drastic change from the amiable Mike Quade. Front-office relationships were deteriorating. Then came a mid-August debacle of a half-hearted, grumbling exhibition performance at The Joe by the A's, where even the most recent graduates who might feel the most warmth toward the old ball yard were distant and uninspired. "A disgrace," Mincher termed it, saying it led to more negative feedback than anything in franchise history. On August 30, the *Times* broke the story that the Stars would be divorcing from Oakland after fourteen seasons.

Keith Lieppman, the A's farm director and now a member of the organization for a half century as a player, manager and official, said: "It's hard to discard all the good things that have happened in Huntsville. Unfortunately, toward the end, there was rough times, but for the most part I tend to think about positive things, and they far outweigh the little things that went wrong."

7

THE MILWAUKEE BREWERS ERA

MORE PROSPECTS AND MORE PLAYOFFS

Sal Bando never earned superstar status on a team with Reggie Jackson and Catfish Hunter, but he was the A's captain, a designation he earned at age twenty-five. He was a calming influence in a turbulent clubhouse, an outspoken yet diplomatic critic of owner Charles O. Finley and one heck of a dependable player. Don Mincher was six years older than Bando, but Bando was an old soul, and they clicked when Mincher arrived in Oakland in a 1970 trade.

By the late 1990s, Bando had moved into administration and up the ladder, to the position of general manager of the Milwaukee Brewers. He and Mincher rekindled their relationship through frequent bump-ins at baseball's Winter Meetings, and in early September 1998, Bando reached out to his old teammate with an offer to bring the Brewers club to Huntsville.

"It wasn't a very difficult decision. When I found out Milwaukee was willing and excited and really wanted to come here, it pretty much made up my mind," Mincher said. He was swayed by Milwaukee's emphasis on player development, on its new stadium that would certainly boost the big club's investment in talent and, finally, by the Brewers' membership in the National League. Huntsville fans could easily see graduates play in person nearby in Atlanta and could see them frequently on the two TV superstations of the day, WGN in Chicago and TBS in Atlanta, both of which broadcast their teams' full schedules.

The Stars' new marriage shared the front of the sports page with some other big news. In the ninth inning of a game in St. Louis, former Star

Mark McGwire hit his 63rd home run of the season, having surpassed Roger Maris's all-time record of 61 just a week earlier.

The fourteen years of the Oakland era produced a 1,029-961 regular-season record, with two championships and eight trips to the playoffs; the latter was an almost effortless 3-game sweep of Leonard's team at the hands of Mobile in 1998. The sixteen-year Milwaukee partnership led to one pennant (shared with Jacksonville when the 2001 playoffs were canceled) and six playoff trips, including consecutive years of losing in the finals.

In the player-development, made-it-big-in-the-show aspect, Milwaukee was equal to Oakland. The magical names of Canseco and McGwire put every future Star in their shadow. Guys like Tim Hudson and Terry Steinbach were terrific. But Milwaukee could counter with Ryan Braun (2011 NL MVP), Prince Fielder (319 homers in an injury-shortened career), Lorenzo Cain (2014 ALCS MVP), Nelson Cruz (seven-time All-Star and second to Miguel Cabrera in homers among active players going into the 2023 season), J.J. Hardy and Michael Brantley.

The answer to a trivia question showed up to manage the Huntsville Stars in 1999. Who was on first base when Hank Aaron hit his record-breaking 715th home run on April 8, 1974?

Darrell Evans was a breath of fresh air, friendly and accessible. Such was the contrast from Jeffrey Leonard that any press box inhabitant who made obvious observations comparing the two managers were levied a 25¢ fine, collected in an old mayonnaise jar. Mincher was so amused by the kitty that he offered to match the total at season's end, and ultimately a charitable donation of nearly $250 was made.

At the midpoint, the Brewers promoted a hulking first baseman from A ball who seemed totally outmatched. Though Bucky Jacobsen hit well below his weight at .193, he came back in 2000 with 18 homers, 50 RBIs and a .276 average before breaking his wrist in July. (Healthy again the next year, he would mash 10 homers, drive in 28 RBIs and bat .441 in 27 games before being promoted to Triple A. By 2004, he enjoyed a meteoric bit of stardom with the Mariners.)

Ben Sheets made only 13 starts for Huntsville in 2000 but left his mark with a 5-3 record and a skinny 1.88 ERA. Months later, he left his mark

Nelson Cruz, seen here in 2005, went from Huntsville to a long, prolific major-league career. *Courtesy Alabama Media Group.*

Catcher Brian Moon (*left*) relaxes with Ben Sheets in 2001. Sheets pitched for the Stars and pitched in the gold-medal game for Team USA in the 2000 Olympics. *Courtesy Milwaukee Brewers.*

internationally. The affable right-hander from Louisiana pitched a 3-hit shutout against Cuba in the Summer Olympics to win the gold medal for Team USA.

The team aces that year were Travis Smith (12-7) and Derek Lee (11-3, 2.54 ERA). The latter was actually Robert D. Lee and was inevitably tagged "The General." Lee was something of a Rocky Coyle of Stars' pitchers, an uber-popular hard worker who was inexplicably never given a big-league shot by the Brewers. Lee spent parts of five seasons in Huntsville—"The Mayor" became a replacement nickname for "The General"—and left with more wins (42) and arguably more friends than any Huntsville pitcher ever.

The final game of the 2000 season showcased the versatility of Jared Mathis, a two-time Rocky Award winner from the Huntsville fans. The Floridian played all nine positions in the September 4 game and even scored the game-winning run on a Toby Kominek single.

Following consecutive losing records, the Stars won the 2001 first-half division title and beat Birmingham in the Western Division playoffs. Manager Ed Romero's team was stocked with veteran players who may have fallen off the *Baseball America* top-prospect radar but played hard and were productive, notably twenty-six-year-old Dave Gibraltar and twenty-seven-year-old Josh Klimek. Jacksonville was in Huntsville to open the championship series on September 11, the day of the terrorist attacks. The series was canceled, and the Stars and Suns were declared co-champions.

In 2003, manager Frank Kremblas's nightly lineup included three of Milwaukee's brightest prospects, shortstop J.J. Hardy and outfielders Corey Hart and Dave Krynzel. But they almost didn't make the Opening Day lineup. On the eve of the season, the *Huntsville Times* thought it'd be a cute photo to have these young prospects, all twenty-one or younger, posed on the swing set the Stars had erected in a short-lived Kids Zone. Hardy, Hart and Krynzel weren't content to simply sit there. They had to begin swinging to see who could go the highest. Suddenly—crack! The frame of the wooden swing set broke under all the weight. Fortunately, the hardware held firmly enough for the threesome to grind things to a halt and eject themselves from the swings—and to help the local newspaper's legal team avoid a most difficult telephone call. With Hart winning MVP honors, that club reached the Southern League finals before losing at Carolina in Game 5.

Good things coming in threes, another trio of highly touted prospects landed in 2004—and were kept off the swing set. Rickie Weeks led the NCAA in hitting in back-to-back seasons and won the prestigious Golden Spikes Award despite playing for unheralded Southern University in Baton Rouge. The Brewers made him the second overall pick in the 2003 draft.

A trio of bright young Stars hit the playground outside Joe Davis Stadium. Corey Hart (*left*), Dave Krynzel (*bottom*) and J.J. Hardy were indicative of Milwaukee's rising developmental program, 2003. *Courtesy Alabama Media Group.*

Along with Weeks came the sons of major-league stars, albeit guys with little else in common. Prince Fielder, still lugging some baby fat, was the Stars' first baseman. Tony Gwynn Jr. was the center fielder. Gwynn enjoyed a warm familial situation, and his voice was a dead ringer for his father, who by that point was a regular on ESPN broadcasts. Fielder's father, Cecil, was a major-league slugger who couldn't control his extravagance, and he and his son were estranged when Prince played in Huntsville. Uncomfortably, Cecil attended several games in Huntsville, often sitting quietly in the press box, then leaving without his son granting him an audience. All three prospects had decent but not dazzling stats, and a team where on-field management was laser-focused on their development rather than winning finished 10 games under .500.

Tony Gwynn Jr., Prince Fielder and Rickie Weeks were centerpieces of the Stars lineup in 2004. *Courtesy Alabama Media Group.*

Another bold-faced name arrived on the scene late in the 2006 season and registered Canseco-like numbers. Ryan Braun, a first-round pick from the University of Miami, had barely 100 games of pro experience when he was promoted to manager Don Money's Huntsville club in early July. He batted .303 with 15 homers and 40 RBIs in 59 games, and the Stars won 36 of their final 47 after a 24-45 start, though they ultimately lost to Montgomery in the championship series.

Ryan Braun led a U-turn of the Stars' fortunes— and took Huntsville to the playoffs in 2006. *Courtesy Alabama Media Group.*

The Stars got a rematch with Montgomery in the 2007 finals, but only after outdueling the Tennessee Smokies in the first round. Mark Holliman of the Smokies threw a seven-inning no-hitter against the Stars in June and even hit a 2-run homer. Corey Thurman, Dave Johnson and Luis Pena got more than a measure of revenge with a combined no-hitter on September 8 in the second game of the playoffs, the only home no-hitter for Huntsville.

Against Montgomery, with the series tied 2 games apiece, the Stars were leading at home going into the ninth inning. On the mound was Pena, who had 12 saves and hadn't given up a homer all year in 35 relief appearances. But Sergio Pedroza, just called up from Class A in time for the playoffs (hello, Justin Bowles!), hit a 3-run, opposite-field homer to take the lead, and the deflated Stars couldn't muster anything in their half of the ninth. Never again would a Stars team reach the championship finals.

AT FIVE FEET, SEVEN inches, Ángel Salomé fit no scout's parameters as a prospect, particularly as a catcher. But in 2008, he batted .360, the best season average in Stars' history. He did so with 132 hits, 45 of those for extra bases. He also memorably dropped to a knee at home plate on May 24 and proposed to his girlfriend, Johanica. He was rewarded with a brief September promotion to Milwaukee but found himself back in the minors in 2009. The Brewers were concerned about his size, thought he had poor footwork and only an average arm. So he made a proposal to the Brewers. After taking a brief leave in early 2010 for the birth of the couple's first child and because he said he was struggling mentally, he requested a move to the outfield. A five-foot, seven-inch corner outfielder is just as rare as a five-seven catcher, and his average plummeted, leading the Brewers to release him.

Milwaukee giving freedom to players with big numbers and big potential was an ongoing theme late in this first decade of the new century, and even into the final days of the marriage with Huntsville. To get C.C. Sabathia for all of 17 appearances in the playoff push in 2008, they traded Michael Brantley and Matt LaPorta, among others. Alcides Escobar, who had a franchise-record 179 hits the same year Salome batted .360, was the ALCS MVP for the Royals in 2015, and Lorenzo Cain won the same award the previous year, when the Brewers sent them to Kansas City for Zack Grienke, who pitched all of 49 games for Milwaukee. Nelson Cruz, still going strong in his forties as of the 2023 season, was traded to Texas by the Brewers in return for two guys with a combined 158 career homers.

The Brewers did make the playoffs in 2011 during Ryan Braun's MVP season, but until a new-look Milwaukee franchise took shape in the late 2010s, no matter the drastic trades (or because of them), they were like a five-foot, seven-inch catcher. They came up short.

Outfielder Lorenzo Cain, 2010. *Courtesy Alabama Media Group.*

8

HUNTER MORRIS

LOCAL BOY DOES GOOD

The scouting reports were being created as early as 1999, when the Brewers sent their first farm club to Huntsville. A five-tool talent. Hitting. Pitching. Savvy.

He was ten years old.

No scouting report could have predicted the future or the remarkable story of how Hunter Morris came to become a professional baseball player and have the most impressive season in Huntsville Stars history, arguably one of the most impressive individual seasons for any athlete in the city's history.

As the first Huntsville-born player for the Stars, Morris won the Southern League MVP award in 2012, leading the league in homers and RBIs. He did so while constantly juggling obligations as team leader, media darling and young father. He did so "with grace, style and humility," said his manager, Darnell Coles.

"He could have put a lot of pressure on himself, but he didn't," outfielder Josh Prince said. "It's going to sound weird when I say this, but he let it go in one ear and out the other, like it was no big deal. Like it's something everybody does. But it's not what everybody does."

Morris acknowledged it was "a unique situation," and there was an abiding family feel to the season. Wife Macie and their son, Tripp, were fixtures at the park. His parents, Linda and Jeff, seldom missed a game. The Stars even created a special Father's Day bobblehead, with Hunter holding Tripp in his arms.

Above, left: Hunter Morris was the face of the franchise for the Stars in his MVP season, 2012. *Courtesy Alabama Media Group.*

Above, right: Hunter Morris, shown in 2012, was the first Huntsville-born player to play for the Stars. *Courtesy Alabama Media Group.*

Right: Darnell Coles, a longtime major leaguer, was a popular manager with the Stars. He is shown here in 2011. *Courtesy Alabama Media Group.*

Morris was not the first local product to play professionally at Joe Davis Stadium. Many had come in as visiting players. Josh Willingham, a humble kid from nearby Florence destined for a splendid major-league career as an outfielder, was a catcher for Carolina when it no-hit the Stars in 2004. ("Did you ever catch one of those?" Willingham gushed to his manager, former big leaguer Ron Hassey, unaware that Hassey had in fact caught

Hunter Morris, 2012. *Courtesy Alabama Media Group.*

perfect games pitched by Len Barker and Dennis Martinez.) Braves farmhand Marc Lewis of Decatur almost singlehandedly beat the slugging '97 Stars in the championship series. And there was a kid who had a good arm but just a passing familiarity with the strike zone as a prepubescent pitcher. Craig Kimbrel pitched the ninth inning of an August 7, 2009 game for the Mississippi Braves, walking the first batter, inducing a double play and then striking out the last man to earn a save. Two years later, he'd be the National League Rookie of the Year.

Morris, an All-State player at Grissom and the SEC Player of the Year in 2010 for Auburn, actually debuted in Huntsville on May 21, 2011, in a four-game call-up from Class A Brevard County. It was a nice appetizer.

In 2012, he batted .303 and had league bests in homers (28), RBIs (113), hits (158), slugging percentage (.563) and total bases (294). He set a Huntsville record for doubles (40) and ended the season in the team's top ten in seven offensive categories. He was awarded a Gold Glove for his defense. The *Huntsville Times* named him its 2012 Sports Person of the Year.

"It was kinda surreal," he said that winter, sitting in a living room cluttered with Tripp's toys. "There was a lot of hard work and frustration that went into the success on the field. But for it to all come to fruition and happen as well as it did, for me to play as well as I did, for it to be the year I happened to be in Huntsville, in one of the toughest leagues in baseball, in a turning point for my career, I'm not sure I could have drawn it up any better."

Hunter Morris's season seemed to be the last without great gloom surrounding the franchise. The Stars finished 59-79 the next year, the fifth consecutive losing season, and averaged only 1,877 fans per game.

To be sure, things had already been growing bleak. During a scouting visit in July 2009, Gord Ash, the Milwaukee Brewers' assistant general manager, sat in the air-conditioned comfort of the press box that overlooked a dismal Sunday afternoon crowd of 660. Huntsville, said Ash, "is a very apathetic baseball town, and something's going to have to change. They're going to be very sorry in a couple of years when they don't have baseball." Rather than it serving as a wake-up call for the casual fan, for city leaders and for owner

Miles Prentice, that widely circulated quote served only to further increase the disdain for the Brewers, whose prospect pipeline had shrunk and who weren't really embraced from Day One. When Prentice held a forty-five-minute meeting with Mayor Tommy Battle two weeks later, he made a plea for a new ballpark and claimed the Stars were a "drain financially."

By 2011, Pat O'Conner, then the president of Minor League Baseball, had made a visit to town and declared, "I have real concerns about the long-term future [of baseball in Huntsville]."

Ultimately, much blame has to rest with E. Miles Prentice III, an attorney based in New York City. Prentice had been stung by Major League Baseball's rejection of his bid to buy the Kansas City Royals but invested in minor-league properties and saw the opportunity to add to his portfolio when the Huntsville Stars' ownership group was looking for a buyer in 2000 on the heels of Mincher's ascension to the Southern League presidency. Prentice tried, and failed again, to add to that portfolio when he made bids to buy the Boston Red Sox and Houston Astros in the 2010s. Perhaps he was daydreaming and looking too far out the window, with plans that were too grandiose, to devote sufficient attention to the Huntsville franchise he bought with such early promise and such high hopes. He planned to keep the team in Huntsville "forever," he said in an interview on the eve of the press conference to announce his purchase. "Forever" turned out to be fourteen years.

Prentice was out of sight, out of touch. During a couple of seasons, he never attended a game in Huntsville. He held a distant relationship with elected officials, fans and media. At a Southern League All-Star Game, in full view of a dozen witnesses, he erupted in a profane tirade about a columnist's critical take on the franchise. Finally, Prentice spewed, "I don't even know who the hell he is." He was calmly informed that the writer in

Miles Prentice bought the Stars in 2001 from the consortium of local owners that kept the team in Huntsville. *Courtesy Alabama Media Group.*

question was the venerable John Pruett—and he might note that the press box at Prentice's team's stadium was named in Pruett's honor.

All this was heartbreaking to Mincher, who had been enamored with Prentice's resume, his business savvy and, mostly, his passion for the game. "You're going to love him," Mincher once told a friend. "He's like us. He's a baseball guy." Or, as Mincher said in the introductory press conference, "Miles is the perfect guy to be here.…He loves baseball as much as any human I've ever seen." Give him credit: Prentice did have that rare knack of avoiding looking like a total nerd when sporting the mixed-up wardrobe look of white Oxford shirt, necktie, Brooks Brothers blue blazer, dress slacks— and a baseball cap. *Forbes* writer Gary Shilling once noted: "I think other people would look kind of presumptuous or goofy or stupid. But with Miles, well, I guess it's just part of Miles." But if he was "a baseball guy," it was seldom revealed within the 256 area code.

In December 2012, baseball's Winter Meetings were held at the Gaylord Opryland Hotel, the sprawling complex in Nashville. Late one afternoon, before a wine-and-dine event hosted by the Milwaukee Brewers, Prentice sat down for a thirty-minute conversation with a Huntsville reporter at the Cascades American Café.

It was occasionally contentious and generally candid. The reporter suggested that Prentice needed to devote an off-season week in Huntsville to engage with business and political leaders. His general manager, Buck Rogers, was a workhorse, but there were doors that only a team owner, not a general manager, could breach. The contrast in Huntsville and his team in Midland, Texas, were illuminated. There was one very telling phrase as the personality of the two cities was discussed: "I can't speak with any authority [about Huntsville]." As for the flaws of Joe Davis Stadium, which had a particularly weather-plagued 2012 season: "The leaks we can't do anything about. You got a big umbrella?" he said.

To be sure, Prentice's absentee ownership wasn't the only factor in the deterioration of what had two decades earlier been considered the model franchise in the Southern League. Affiliating with the Milwaukee Brewers, a franchise with all the glitz and appeal of a used minivan, was not readily accepted by fans. The too-big stadium had grown to feel like a mausoleum, all cold and gray and depressing. The City of Huntsville was a deliberate and frugal landlord. There was poor communication between the city and ownership, with no clear delineation of duties. There was a general apathy toward the team. Huntsville is a fickle and unpredictable spectator market; the night before fewer than 2,000 attended a postseason game that featured a dozen future big leaguers, nearly 7,500 paid twenty-five dollars and up to watch professional wrestling at the Von Braun Center.

The front office was short-staffed. Where Prentice had a dozen full-timers and a half-dozen interns for his Class AA Midland team, the Stars worked with the opposite mathematics. Marketing and promotion was modest—except on nights when it was so embarrassingly immodest. Even *Sports Illustrated* noted the 2011 evening that the Stars hosted "Pleasures Ladies Night," with its pregame party in a skybox and display of products sold by a local adult emporium, on the same night they also hosted the North-Central Alabama Girl Scouts sleepover.

Thus many seasons were clouded by speculation and rumors of an impending sale or move. Prentice began looking for a buyer or new location. Though denying it to reporters, he talked with Madison officials about moving the team there. Eventually, he struck a deal with an ownership group led by Ken Young that would move the team to Biloxi in 2015. There had been no traction for a new park in Huntsville to replace what had become the oldest stadium in the league. Really, the move was the only logical thing to happen.

Barely two weeks into the lame-duck season of 2014, a Harvard graduate named Brent Suter just missed pitching the sixth no-hitter in Stars' history, in front of almost two thousand schoolkids making a field trip to the ballpark. Suter lost his bid to the lead-off hitter in the ninth, much as Huntsville lost a combined no-hitter on a similar Education Day in 2007 with two outs in the ninth.

The team that featured future Seattle Mariners star Mitch Haniger, former Huntsville High pitcher Jed Bradley and an 82-RBI man in Nick Ramirez won the first-half pennant. After dropping the season finale at home to Mississippi, they split the first two games of the North Division playoffs, with a 9–0 win on September 6 in what would be the Stars' final home game. After splitting

Top: Brent Suter, seen here in 2014, nearly pitched a no-hitter for the Stars, then made it big with the Brewers. *Courtesy Alabama Media Group.*

Bottom: Only a few years after pitching for Huntsville High, Jed Bradley was on the mound for the Stars in 2014. *Courtesy Alabama Media Group.*

two more in Chattanooga, Huntsville fell behind, 7–2, to the Lookouts before rallying their way into heartbreak, leaving the tying runner on base with a pair of ninth-inning strikeouts.

However, in 2015, because the Biloxi stadium construction fell way behind schedule, through weather delays and political wrangling, the newly minted Shuckers had to play their first 54 games on the road. That included 15 games in Huntsville, where team ownership still held a lease on Joe Davis Stadium.

On May 25, the Shuckers were the home team against the Birmingham Barons at The Joe. So discombobulated were things in Biloxi, no one could officially say if this would be the final pro game in Huntsville or if the Shuckers would have to make a return trip. The announced attendance was 224 for the Monday afternoon game. Forty years and thirty-six days since fans went in one turnstile and workers spilled out the other, a rainstorm brought the game to an end after four and a half innings. Joe Davis Stadium was left for ghosts, some souvenir seekers, uncontrolled weeds, the ravages of time—and ultimately for a reprieve a half-dozen years later that would assure a facelift and new chapter as home to high school football and pro soccer.

9

TRASH PANDAS

Pro Baseball a Rousing Success in Return

*L*ess than an hour from Miles Prentice's native home in Vermont, a man was doing due diligence on how to purchase a minor-league team. He was following the developments in Huntsville and was especially struck by the headline on a newspaper opinion column he stumbled across in his research: "Losing These Stars Can Be Best Hope for Baseball's Future."

Ralph Nelson was already aware that some of the most successful minor-league franchises were those in cities that had once lost baseball but returned in newer, fresher packaging. All around the South were such examples: Birmingham, Chattanooga, Greenville, Montgomery and even a wonderfully named semipro team called the Savannah Bananas, packing the park in another city Nelson was pondering.

Nelson's CV encompassed so much in baseball, starting on the ground floor with the San Francisco Giants as a PR department assistant, then rising to the position of assistant general manager. He was an architect of the expansion Arizona Diamondbacks and vice-president of umpiring for Major League Baseball. Nelson moonlighted as a college basketball referee, and he created a stats program purchased by the NCAA.

Not on his baseball CV: a minor-league franchise. But he often thought back to an evening at the Pink Pony steakhouse, a spring training baseball mecca in Scottsdale, and a conversation there with Bing Devine, a fixture in the game.

"Ralph, I'm going to tell you something. You want to have a great career in baseball? I know you're going to have a great career in the major leagues.

But finish your career by owning a minor league team in a small or mid-sized city," Devine said. "It's the most satisfying thing you can do in our business. It is the most fulfilling experience you can have. The fans are great. The players are great. I'm telling you, that's what you need to do."

In a process vastly more complex than can be described in one paragraph, Nelson enlisted a band of investors, purchased the Mobile BayBears, obtained permission to transfer them to Madison, met with landowner Louis Breland and others to determine a stadium site, hired a staff, fired some of the staff, hired some more, convinced the City of Madison to build a stadium, hired a broadcaster (third-generation announcer Josh Caray), conducted a groundbreaking ceremony attended by hundreds, signed a working agreement with the Los Angeles Angels, introduced the inaugural manager (former All-Star shortstop Jay Bell) and found a naming-rights partner in Toyota.

Along the way, Nelson, so skilled in massaging the media, stoked the hype machine. Not far from the stadium that drew 244 for the last pro baseball game, ten times that many showed up at Big Spring Park for an unveiling of the team uniforms. A contest was created to name the team, won by Matthew Higley's nomination of Trash Pandas, with the announcement made on live TV. Trash Panda—slang for a raccoon—was amplified by the San Diego–based marketing firm Brandiose to become this grand symbol of all things Huntsville, noting that the raccoon was among the best problem-solvers of all God's creatures. And who has exemplified problem-solving more than the ingenious human engineering minds of north Alabama, where raccoons are plentiful?

What Nelson—or anyone—was not prepared for was a global pandemic. The Trash Pandas were targeting their April 15, 2020 home debut, and Nelson had put together a solid staff, led by general manager Garrett Fahrmann and assistant GM Lindsey Knupp. It was heartbreaking when the opener was postponed and, eventually, the entire season canceled. Inspired by Knupp's creativity and a sense of teamwork and purpose, the Trash Pandas' staff cobbled together a calendar of events that opened the doors to the stadium and maintained a decent revenue stream despite the absence of baseball.

But what's that cliché about having to break eggs to make an omelet? That certainly had become the case with Nelson, whether it was staff morale or feuds with Madison mayor Paul Finley or decisions questioned by the ownership group, BallCorps. What was charismatic and contagious enthusiasm to some was bombast and off-putting to others. On April 21,

Garrett Fahrmann, Rocket City's vice-president and GM, took over the club under challenging circumstances only weeks before the 2021 season debut. *Courtesy Rocket City Trash Pandas.*

2021, with Opening Day so close you could almost taste the hot dogs and nachos, Nelson announced his resignation as team president and CEO, saying he was going to focus his energy on another minor-league team he wanted to relocate.

Finley got in the last licks in a statement from the city: "Every organization is larger than one person, and our Rocket City Trash Pandas have an incredible staff ready to welcome our community into Toyota Field May 11th....Let's 'Play Ball!'"

Alas, May 11 failed to provide a storybook ending. After losing four of six in a road series, the Trash Pandas dropped an extra-inning game to Tennessee because of a botched attempt fielding a bunt. There were some growing pains. The players hadn't seen live action in a year. The roster was a cocktail of ingredients brought in from other organizations, the tacit indication of the weakness and shallowness of the Angels' farm system. Jay Bell, the first major-league acquisition of the expansion Diamondbacks in the days Ralph Nelson was helping construct that team, did a masterful and patient job managing his team and the revolving door that 2021 brought. In a season that started late and ended prematurely because of COVID, fifty-nine different players saw action. Two others were on

The stands were still filling up as teams were introduced at the inaugural home game. *Courtesy Rocket City Trash Pandas*.

Longtime major leaguer Jay Bell was the Trash Pandas' first manager. *Courtesy Rocket City Trash Pandas*.

the roster, awaiting their debuts, when the season was canceled with four games remaining.

The season ended with a masterful one-hitter from Christopher Molina, beating Pensacola, 4–0. Molina struck out 11 in eight innings, par for the course for the Trash Pandas' staff. They whiffed 1,112 opposing batters, the best ratio in the league.

Rocket City was the microcosm for the new game of baseball, of power hitting and power pitching. The Trash Pandas hit a league-best 152 homers. With 90 of those at home and 61 by the visitors, Toyota Field saw more homers than any park in Double A South.

Mitch Nay, the league's coleader in homers with 23, was named to the All-Star team. David MacKinnon, the fan favorite first baseman, should have been. He batted .285 with 13 homers and a league-leading 65 RBIs. Izzy Wilson mashed 21 homers and stole 25 bases, and Luis Aviles hit 11 homers in the month of July alone, driving in 28 runs.

Their 54-56 record merits an asterisk. They were at one point 53-48 before an injury-depleted, inexperienced roster endured an eight-game losing streak in September as the pennant race began.

And, well, there were the fans. It didn't take long for the preseason upheaval and early season hiccups to become forgotten. "Two or three weeks later, the

David MacKinnon was the unquestioned leader of the 2021 Trash Pandas. *Courtesy Rocket City Trash Pandas.*

The Trash Pandas quickly became no. 1 in the hearts of Huntsville-area fans. *Courtesy Rocket City Trash Pandas.*

thoughts of money went away when I saw all the smiling faces and happy people. What I recognized was the asset we had with Double A baseball, that it's back," Finley said.

The Trash Pandas drew 274,858 in just forty-eight home dates, the best in Double A ball. Only four times in thirty seasons did the Stars top that figure, and that with the benefit of full, 70-game home slates. The Trash Pandas sold millions in merchandise. They also raised more than $100,000 for local charities through various promotions.

Maybe the premature cancelation because of COVID was an appropriate bookend to the Trash Pandas' inaugural-season saga. But the resilience of the Rocket City staff, the team's myriad success stories, the magical moments and the delirious fans were neatly summed up in one Trash Pandas' season-ending headline. It was so appropriate for an area in which the debut of one team was compared to a moon landing. "Mission Accomplished," it read.

WHEN DON MINCHER SERVED as the Huntsville Stars' general manager, he was chided by team owner Larry Schmittou for having expended all of the grace from the Baseball Gods in one season. The Stars of 1985 won the pennant, set attendance records and boasted the league MVP in the redoubtable José Canseco.

Andy Schatzley was named SL Manager of the Year after leading Rocket City to a dominant season in 2022. *Courtesy Rocket City Trash Pandas.*

It would be easy to parallel the 2021 Rocket City Trash Pandas with the original Stars, and the grace of the Baseball Gods. But, whatdoyouknow—there was a spectacular encore season awaiting in 2022.

First, at the turnstiles. The Trash Pandas averaged 5,031 fans per game over 65 regular-season home dates. That was tops in the Southern League and eighth among the 30 Class AA franchises. If you were among the 327,007 who found your way into Toyota Field, chances are you saw a Trash Pandas victory. The club was 49-20 at home, the most home victories in all of minor-league baseball.

Overall, the club was 81-57, winning both halves in the Southern League North behind SL Manager of the Year Andy Schatzley, a thirty-eight-year-old Arkansan managing at the highest level of his career. He was blessed with having 14 of the top 30 prospects in the Angels' system, as ranked by mlb.com. Alas, the Trash Pandas were eliminated by the Tennessee Smokies—a team they dominated the prior season—in the North Division playoffs. The Trash Pandas won the opener in Tennessee, 9–5, but were swept at home, 4–2 and 3–1.

While the Trash Pandas thrived in 2022, their fans kept an eager and proud eye on the major leagues, where numerous Rocket City graduates were earning promotions to the Los Angeles Angels and often making substantial contributions, none more so than Reid Detmers, the Angels' first-round draft pick and the starting pitcher for the 2021 home debut of the Trash Pandas. On May 10, Detmers pitched a no-hitter against Tampa Bay. Said Detmers to reporters: "It's just something I've dreamed ever since I was a little kid. I didn't think it would ever happen."

10

GABBY STREET
TO CRAIG KIMBREL

A LONG LIST OF HUNTSVILLE-BORN BASEBALL STARS

*T*he Ripley-esque feat prompted all variety of reaction from folks, from awestruck fans to the occasional amateur Galileo who wanted to apply mathematics and physics to something that seemed to have been birthed as a bar bet.

What happened on August 21, 1908, ensured a noteworthy footnote to the long baseball career of Huntsville-born Charles Evard "Gabby" Street.

Street spent seven years in the majors as a light-hitting catcher (.208, 2 homers in 1,501 at bats). As Hall of Famer Walter Johnson told the Associated Press, "You don't see Gabby's kind of a catcher anymore. He never hit much, but what a receiver he was—big fellow, a perfect target, great arm, slow afoot, but spry as a cat on his feet behind the plate, always talking, always hustling, full of pep and fight,"

Following his playing career, Street managed the St. Louis Cardinals for four seasons and the St. Louis Browns for one season, then became a beloved, familiar radio voice for Midwest baseball fans. Said his broadcast partner, Harry Caray, "No pompous, self-righteous guy, Gabby Street, no siree sir; but all human being instead, warm and mellow and friendly."

In such esteem was he regarded, the Gabby Street Youth Baseball League was established in his adopted hometown of Joplin, Missouri, where he died in 1951 at age sixty-eight. (Joplin was also moved to name a street in his honor, but that led to some debate and complications. As in, how odd would Gabby Street Street sound? Ultimately, a roadway that had already

Gabby Street. *Courtesy Huntsville Public Library.*

been designated a "boulevard' was chosen for re-titling, enabling a less clunky moniker.)

When his unfortunate and untimely passing was marked, more than a few obituaries indeed included the phrase, "Former major league catcher Charles 'Gabby' Street, who once caught a ball dropped from the Washington Monument...."

That parenthetical phrase hardly defined Street's career, but it heaped upon him a lifetime of notoriety.

Imagine how such an event would occur these days. Live ESPN coverage. Breathless analysts. Interviews with Weather Channel pundits. Cruel tweets as attempt after attempt failed. Boxes full of government red tape to access the monument for such frivolity. A title sponsor, surely an insurance company, considering the potential for mayhem.

Instead, two Washington gentlemen—John Biddle and Preston Gibson—were debating the possibility of catching a baseball dropped from the Washington Monument. They enlisted Street, then catching for the Washington Senators. Depending on the report, Street either helped settle their $500 bet or had some money on the line himself. News of the attempt was leaked to one Washington newspaper, the *Evening Star*, which dispatched a reporter to the scene and took "exclusive" ownership of the story—an exclusive that lasted less than twenty-four hours.

Street stationed himself at the base of the monument's south side, better to be shielded against the sun. Gibson went to the top of the monument, 550 feet above ground level, with a sack full of baseballs. A small chute was extended from a window, and a baseball was rolled down the chute and out into a brisk breeze. Several times, the balls were blown back against the tapered monument and bounced away, well out of reach. Finally, Gibson simply lobbed them out, allowing for some clearance.

"I could not see the ball until it had come down some distance," Street would write in a first-person sidebar in the *Washington Post*. "I was given a signal when each was thrown, but could not see it until it was almost halfway down. Then it seemed to be that the ball was waving. For a time it was impossible to get near the ball, which was either hitting the monument or falling so close to it that it was impossible for me to get with it."

Eventually, Street moved to the north side of the monument, where the wind was less troublesome. On the twelfth attempt, Street got his mitt on the ball but "was a bit timid" and didn't hold on.

Thirteen was the lucky catch. He hung on to the ball that, according to science or speculation, was traveling some 135 feet per second and hit his glove at ninety-five miles per hour (mph). It was equal to catching a 117-pound weight being dropped 1 foot.

"The ball did not seem to hit the glove any harder than some of those fast ones Walter Johnson serves up....When we went around to the north side, I found it easy, and when I succeed in getting under the ball, which looked about as big as a chestnut, but felt as heavy as a ton of coal, I froze on," Street said in another first-person sidebar, this one in the *Washington Herald*, further spoiling the *Star*'s exclusivity.

However, such were deadlines and print cycles that Street's catch came hot off the *Star* presses early on the afternoon of August 21, and some fans en route to the Senators' home game that day against Detroit were already privy to the news—and to the *Star*'s hyperbolic reportage, at a time when editorial standards for sensitivity were obviously a little more relaxed: "Charlie, who really doesn't look strong enough to catch cold, not only got the ball in his mitt but also held on to it like grim death to an India famine sufferer."

The monument delivery wasn't the last ninety-plus-mph delivery Street would see that day. He caught a 5-hit, 3–1 victory pitched by the immortal Walter Johnson. The Tigers' only run came on a double steal, after Street fired to second baseman Bob Unglaub then dropped Unglaub's return throw—made from ground level 127 feet away.

Gabby was one of seven children of Williams and Sis Street. He played baseball for his Huntsville school team and on the sandlots. By the age of twelve, he was already playing with grown-up teammates on a semipro club called the Milligan Sluggers. He then found his way to South Kentucky College in Hopkinsville, a now-defunct school with fewer than three hundred students when Street arrived. However, it led to a wonderful quirk of fate. Hopkinsville had joined the Class D Kitty (Kentucky-Illinois-Tennessee) League, and he signed for a sixty-dollar-a-month contract in 1903. A year later, he reached the big leagues with Cincinnati, taking advantage of the opportunity presented when Branch Rickey refused to play on Sundays. Rickey, later the architect of baseball's farm system, would become Street's boss years later as the general manager of the Cardinals.

Street briefly played for the Boston Beaneaters, then skipped around in the minors, including a stop in San Francisco, where he was jarred from his bed by the massive April 1906 earthquake that killed nearly three thousand and left two hundred thousand homeless. Thus he was relieved to find employment in Williamsport, Pennsylvania, which led to his signing with the Senators. He spent four years with the Senators, then returned to the minors before his career was interrupted by World War I. He served in the U.S. Army and was awarded a Purple Heart after being struck in the leg with a bullet fired from a German aircraft.

After Armistice Day, a return to the majors as a player was far-fetched. So Street embarked on a career as a coach and manager. At one of those stops, he met his future wife, Lucinda, in Joplin, in the deep southwest corner of Missouri. He and Lucinda had two children, Charles Jr. and Sally.

In 1929, Street was finally back in the majors, coaching the Cardinals. The next season, Rickey installed the forty-seven-year-old Street as the manager. The club went 92-62, winning 21 of its last 25 games to climb from fourth place to the pennant. The next season, the Cards were 1931 World Series champs after a 101-win regular season. He brought that club to Huntsville for a preseason exhibition in April, initially scheduled to face the former Springers, but when that club was disbanded, a gaggle of the top local amateur and semipro talent was put together to face the Cardinals. Box scores are nonexistent, but it's said that Street briefly caught in that game and Dizzy Dean was on the mound. Despite the success in 1931, the Cardinals had some powerful personalities, like Dean, Pepper Martin and Leo Durocher. They'd soon jell as the colorful "Gashouse Gang," which prided itself on dirty uniforms and iconoclastic behavior, and things began to sour for Street. He resigned as manager midway through the 1933 season, managed several minor-league teams, then joined the Browns as manager in 1938.

By then, live radio broadcasts had supplanted the old method of re-creating games in a studio, where the announcer would embellish the play-by-play that clattered in via ticker tape. It was the perfect platform for Street.

He began broadcasting the Browns' games, offering his colorful, loquacious touch, then moved to the Cardinals' broadcast team in 1945, helping usher in a young whippersnapper named Harry Caray. He was on the air through the 1950 season, when poor health began to catch up with him.

At Street's death on February 16, 1951, Caray offered a long tribute on the air. In part, he said: "All that keeps running through my mind are a million miscellaneous things that would hardly be of interest to you, possibly—that lovable laugh, for example; that philosophy of life. I was associated with Gabby going onto seven years, but we didn't work a single day together. We just laughed, lived and argued. 'Can you imagine,' he used to say, 'can you imagine getting paid for all the fun we are having?'"

What a grander, more appropriate eulogy than simply the parenthetical phrase, "who caught a baseball dropped from the Washington Monument." Imagine what it would have been like to know Gabby Street.

Making Connections: Lena Styles

The *Philadelphia Inquirer* byline—Jim Nasium—was the first hint that the strictest journalistic standards were not about to follow in the ensuing paragraphs. With the Philadelphia Athletics hopelessly buried in last place in mid-September 1919, winners of only 33 of their first 123 games, manager Connie Mack filled his lineup card with rookies recently promoted from the minor-league Atlanta Crackers. Or, as Nasium called them, "our callow youths from the underbrush."

Among the callow youths was a Gurley native named Williams Graves "Lena" Styles, making his debut on September 10 against Ty Cobb and the Detroit Tigers. It is but a footnote in Styles's long and colorful history that Mack pinch-hit for him in the bottom of the ninth, and a Philly veteran smacked a walk-off home run. Four days later, Styles got his first big-league hit, against the Chicago White Sox of Shoeless Joe Jackson, Buck Weaver, Eddie Collins and Chick Gandil. A week later, many of those White Sox gathered in a New York hotel room to concoct their plan to throw the 1919 World Series.

Styles, born in November 1899, had something of a Forest Gump nature to his career; perhaps appropriate, since he, too, studied at the University of Alabama. Connie Mack as a manager. Ty Cobb as a first-game opponent. Then the Black Sox. Then, back in the minors, he caught future Hall of Famer Carl Hubbell in an exhibition game against Babe Ruth's Yankees. His last game was in 1931, as a teammate of Leo Durocher, against the Cardinals and manager Gabby Street.

In a 2020 profile of Styles, longtime Anniston journalist Phillip Tutor wrote, "Styles wasn't a character on a par with the rascally Cobb, but Lord was he close." As he bounced between the majors and minors, he was equally a treasured addition to the team and a nuisance. He was a guide for pitchers and versatile enough to have played all defensive positions in the 1922 season in Baltimore. However, before the season began, he held out for a larger contract then was twice arrested on the same night for being drunk and disorderly after an exhibition game in Winston-Salem. "The 'corn-likker,' which finds a ready sale in spite of the Volstead act, had found a ready consumer in the Oriole catcher," reported the *Baltimore Sun*.

As Tutor reported, Styles had another run-in with authorities when he was arrested for trying to hit a Winston-Salem waiter in 1922 and again in 1923, when he and a teammate were drunk at a banquet hosted by Baltimore civic clubs to honor the Orioles. Though Baltimore ownership called him a "bad actor," he was a heck of a hitter.

Perhaps maturity and sobriety caught up with Styles, as he joined the Newark Bears as a twenty-four-year-old, batting .304, including a late-season walk-off single to beat the Orioles. He hit no worse than .282 his next four seasons and was back in the majors in 1930, albeit as the third-string catcher for the Cincinnati Reds. He played more regularly in 1932, but when the Reds traded for future Hall of Famer Ernie Lombardi in 1933, Styles was back in the minors. The one-time bad actor took on the responsibility of being a player-manager in 1934 in Pine Bluff, Arkansas. He spent two years there, then moved to Greenville, Mississippi, for two more seasons, never finishing worse than fourth.

Bill Deyo, a mover and shaker in Anniston who was directly descended from the city's founder and a prep-school classmate of John F. Kennedy, was the president of the Anniston Rams. He hired Styles to manage the club in 1938, its first season in the Southeastern League, then proclaimed, "We'll have a club here that will give the people a run for their money."

"Except they didn't," as Tutor wrote. The Rams were bound for a 62-86 record, and Styles resigned on July 13, saying it was in the best interest of the team and his own health. He opened a tire business in Anniston before returning to Gurley, joining his father, J.E., in operating what was described as a "model farm" in eastern Madison County. He was a popular storyteller and a natural-born performer who participated in plays and musicals. Indeed, there he was, thirty years after being booted from one fancy event, captured at another whoop-de-do event by a *Huntsville Times* photographer. The bow-tied Styles was joined behind a microphone by two other men in serenading a crowd of 250 as part of the Grace Club Auxiliary Follies talent show in 1953.

When Styles died in March 1956 after an extended illness, such was his renown that his death was reported on page one of the newspaper. The phrase "baseball star of yesteryears" hardly did justice to the one-time rascal who had become a pillar of the community.

RAW TALENT: JIM TABOR

On July 4, 1939, in front of 61,808 fans and a brace of his former teammates, a dying man walked reluctantly to a microphone and delivered the most famous speech in baseball history. Lou Gehrig, his body wracked with a disease that would later become inexorably tied to his name, offered words that literally echoed through the cavernous Yankee Stadium—and have echoed in our conscience for eighty years through the magic of Hollywood and baseball lore.

Jim "Rawhide" Tabor debuted with the Red Sox alongside Ted Williams. *Huntsville Public Library.*

Gehrig didn't want to speak that day. He had asked the public address announcer to offer a few words on his behalf. But urged to the microphone, a weeping Gehrig spoke of his "bad break."

Then, the immortal line: "Today, I consider myself the luckiest man on the face of the earth."

Gehrig, who played in 2,130 consecutive games, was thirty-six. In less than two years, he would succumb to amyotrophic lateral sclerosis.

One hundred miles southwest, as Lou Gehrig Appreciation Day was being celebrated in New York, a rookie was slashing his way into baseball prominence, already hinting at immortality, the hottest man in baseball on that particular July 4.

Jim Tabor was arguably the greatest all-around pure baseball talent from the Huntsville area, including the long major-league career of Don Mincher and the spectacular skills of Condredge Holloway, who opted for football rather than accept a $100,000 bonus offer from Montreal in 1971. Mincher laughed through the years that his father, George, even proclaimed Jim Tabor the best player ever from the area, giving an unneeded dose of humility to the ever-modest Mincher.

Described frequently as a "rawboned" youngster from New Hope, Alabama, Tabor was a Boston Red Sox third baseman in 1939. With a fellow rookie named Ted Williams, optimists among the Red Sox faithful were already beginning to imagine a one-two punch that might compare to Babe Ruth and Gehrig. Tabor batted .316 in a 19-game late-season call-up as a twenty-one-year-old in 1938, and Williams was en route to a league-leading 145 RBIs as a rookie in 1939.

In a doubleheader sweep of the Philadelphia Athletics at Shibe Park on July 4, 1939, Williams had 4 RBIs. But that was nothing compared to a day that would live as the pinnacle of Jim Tabor's career.

Tabor, batting seventh in the lineup, hit 4 home runs in the doubleheader. He had one in the opener, then sandwiched an inside-the-park job between a pair of grand slams in the nightcap. He became only the second man in baseball history to sock two grand slams in the same game and only the third to collect four homers in a doubleheader. Gushed the *Boston Globe*, "Gangling Cowboy Jim went to town with his big bat and emerged from what was nothing short of a slight case of murder as the co-holder of two of baseball's outstanding home run records."

He was 2 RBIs shy of Tony Lazzeri's major-league record, a mark he might have reached had he not misread a signal from manager Joe Cronin in the fourth inning and bunted. "Honestly," he told reporters gathered at his locker after the game, "I didn't know I was chasing any records until you writers told me just now." Tabor gave partial credit for a hitting surge to using a lighter bat, one he said he "snitched" from Cleveland's Ken Keltner earlier in the season.

Bases-loaded homers seemed to be a Tabor trademark. As a minor leaguer in 1937, he tagged Bob Feller for a grand slam, and his first major-league homer was a grand slam at Shibe Park in 1938 during his brief call-up.

The Red Sox bullied the Athletics, 17–7 and 18–12, in the doubleheader, as Boston had 35 hits, including 7 homers. There was, you might suspect, no shortage of references to fireworks after this July 4 outing. (However, the Philadelphia media was elsewhere noting a lack of fireworks that day. Pennsylvania had just enacted strict rules against the personal use of fireworks, and the *Philadelphia Inquirer* celebrated in a page-one story that no one in the state was killed or blinded by fireworks in 1939, after 8 deaths, 10 blindings and more than 1,600 statewide injuries in 1938.)

Tabor's performance was treated as a "redemption" story. On June 26, Cronin suspended him for violation of team rules, for the second time that season. According to the manager, Tabor "foolishly broke training much after the fashion of a high school boy who wanted to show off." Off-the-field issues and a reputation as a bit of a rounder would continue to plague Tabor throughout his career.

Thirty years after his feat, the *Boston Globe* published a letter about Tabor that addressed his reputation:

Jim Tabor wasn't a smooth character. People loved him, yet he was a loner.
He didn't have a business head in the sense that he socked away his earnings for a rainy day. He was a soft touch for the fellow who was down, and often loaned more than half his monthly earnings before ever reaching home….He was delighted to see a fellow back on his feet.

I assure you Tabor was no fool; he had what you might call nowadays "soul." He did like to drink, nobody could deny that….Jim Tabor was a man's man and never knew how to be a hypocrite. He married a local girl and fathered two children, a boy and a girl, all of whom he was devoted to.

Above all, he loved baseball…in my opinion he belongs among the greats.

The letter was signed by Virginia Tabor Paro, Jim's daughter.

James Reubin Tabor was born on November 5, 1916, to John H. and Amy Olene Tabor. They lived on a farm between Owens Cross Roads and New Hope, where the elder Tabor was a schoolteacher. He had also been a terrific baseball player as a young man but chose marriage over a potential pro career. The Tabors raised three sons, and each played on an amateur team in New Hope for which their father served as manager and catcher.

Jim was a multisport standout at New Hope High and earned a scholarship offer to play basketball at the University of Alabama. Once on campus, the baseball staff learned of his talent there and swayed him to come out for the team. Following his freshman year, he went off to play semipro ball—then permissible by college rules—and had his first run-in with authority. He butted heads with his manager and was sent packing, but Alabama officials found him another team, and he dazzled there, earning a contract offer from the Philadelphia Athletics with a $3,500 bonus. The Red Sox topped that with a $4,000 offer, and it was agreed that Tabor wouldn't turn professional until he completed his studies at Alabama. However, he lost interest in his studies and by the spring of his sophomore year dropped out. Though the Red Sox encouraged him to stay in school, they sent him to Little Rock in the Southern Association. It was a huge leap from the sandlots of Madison County and college ball, where he'd been only a year earlier, but he batted .295, drove in 94 runs and impressed scouts and Red Sox staff. His speed, arm, hustle and competitive nature were evident to everyone.

Tabor was first coupled with Williams in 1938 with the Minneapolis Millers, and it was an occasionally combustible relationship. Once, the notoriously moody Williams got into a pout and Tabor began punching him, leaving it to their manager to break up a fight.

Bringing Tabor and Williams into the majors together in 1939—on a team that would have four future Hall of Famers in the lineup—was a calculated risk. As Cronin told Boston reporters, "We will be gambling at third base and in right field…but, at least, we'll be gambling with two of the finest young players in the country."

Both lived up to the hype. Tabor delivered at the plate and showed good fielding skills at third. His arm was a cannon, so much so that first baseman Jimmie Foxx reinforced his glove. Tabor committed 40 errors as a rookie, most on throws that endangered the populace in the first base box seats. He batted .289, his 95 RBIs were fourth on the team and he led the club in stolen bases.

He followed with a .285/21/81 line in 1940. After a July 14 doubleheader, in which he went 4-for-8, he married Irene Bryan, a Boston woman with whom he'd have two children, Jim Jr. and Virginia. Marriage agreed with him. He hit 4 homers in the next 3 games, going 6-for-12. But his season was cut short by an appendectomy in August.

Despite his marriage, Tabor still had his wild moments. As former teammate Doc Cramer said in the book *Fenway* by Peter Golenbock, "Jim Tabor was a twister. He would drink, get drunk and be half-drunk when he came to the park." Other teammates were discouraged by his propensity for public drinking, rather than keeping it in the confines of a team hotel, as many did. The Red Sox briefly put private detectives on his tail, thinking that might slow him down. By spring training of 1941, there was more time in Cronin's doghouse, with yet another suspension. Nonetheless, he batted .279 with 16 homers and 101 RBIs that season before a slight slump to .252/17/75 in 1942.

The numbers continued to erode, even as the quality of opposition in wartime was considerably less. Too much drinking? Or too much wear and tear from hard slides on sandpaper-rough infields? From grueling train rides from city to city to daytime midsummer doubleheaders? A combination of them all?

After Tabor enlisted in the U.S. Army and missed the 1945 season, the Phillies purchased his contract from the Red Sox, for whom Tabor had 90 homers and 517 RBIs in six-plus seasons—4 of those homers and 9 of those RBIs on one spectacular afternoon in Philadelphia.

As Maurice Bouchard noted in a piece for the Society for American Baseball Research, the *Boston Globe* sent Tabor south with a less-than-flattering eulogy. "[Tabor] looked like a sure-fire big league star. He was very fast, had power at bat and while erratic of throwing arm, appeared to be about ready to blossom into stardom at any time. Annually, he failed to live up to this promise."

At twenty-nine, he was in the twilight of his career with Philly. Despite a hot start—and the benefit of playing in Shibe Park, the site of his historic day—he never matched his Bosox numbers. The Phillies released him after two seasons, but he found work in the Pacific Coast League. He played solidly for Sacramento but again found himself running afoul of his manager and was briefly suspended. Then, before the 1951 season, Sacramento signed former American League All-Star Ken Keltner, the same man who had famously ended Joe DiMaggio's hitting streak in 1941 with a pair of stupendous defensive plays—and from whom Tabor had "snitched" that lightweight bat that led to 4 homers in one day.

Tabor was shifted to first base and showed some flashes at the plate. But time, injury and hard living had taken their toll. He last played in 1952, then returned to Sacramento, where he began work for a construction company.

Tabor was in Sacramento when he died on August 22, 1953, after suffering a heart attack. He was thirty-six, the same age as Lou Gehrig on the day he proclaimed himself the luckiest man on the face of the earth.

HUNTSVILLE'S MR. BASEBALL: DON MINCHER

Donald Ray Mincher grew up in the Lincoln Mill area, and old-timers still proclaim him one of the best all-around athletes in the city's history. He even received a football scholarship offer to Alabama from soon-to-be-fired coach J.B. "Ears" Whitworth. "The second year," Mincher said, "I would have gotten Bear Bryant as a coach and he'd have probably run me off the second day."

Mincher instead signed a contract with the Chicago White Sox in 1956 and caught a train for Duluth, Minnesota, lugging a suitcase packed by his mother, Lillian, with a Bible right on top of the neatly folded clothes. He was barely eighteen and quickly grew homesick. His father, George, a welder who helped build the cage for the chimpanzee astronaut Ham, was sympathetic but firm when Don phoned home one day. "You made a commitment. You have class. You signed with those people and promised to give them one year and that's what you'll do."

He spent a season and a half in Duluth, then knocked the cover off the ball at two more stops before being traded by the White Sox to the Senators on the eve of the 1960 season for the aging five-time All-Star Roy Sievers.

Don Mincher, 2002. *Courtesy Alabama Media Group.*

After an 0-for-6 start, he doubled off Milt Pappas in his third game, his first major-league hit.

The Senators moved to Minnesota the following year, and he became a fixture there. The Twins won the American League pennant in 1965—his wife, Pat, still has the jersey that Don was wearing during the pennant-clinching celebration—and reached the World Series.

On October 6, 1965, the pitching-rich Los Angeles Dodgers were in Minnesota for Game 1. George and Lillian arrived for the game, and Don and Pat met them for breakfast near their hotel. Don "never said one word," Pat recalled.

Minnesota was trailing, 1–0, in the second inning when Mincher came to bat with two outs and the fearsome Don Drysdale on the mound. Drysdale threw a sinker down and away. Ball one. Then a fastball, waist-high on the inside half of the plate. Mincher turned on the pitch and launched it into the right-field stands, becoming only the fourth man to hit a home run in his first World Series at bat.

Years later, he admitted that after a quick but calm home-run trot, he reached the dugout and: "I started shaking. All of a sudden it hit me what I had done, in front of possibly everybody I knew looking on….That one defining three minutes, it's just forever in my mind."

After the 8–2 beatdown, Drysdale snarled, "My sister could have hit that pitch." In the opposite locker room, Mincher shrugged, "You've still got to hit it when a Hall of Famer throws it."

After Mincher dressed, he joined his family in a waiting room in the basement of the stadium. They embraced, and Don noticed tears rolling down his father's face. His own eyes misting at the retelling, Don said, "It was the first time I ever saw my father cry." Then, trying to bring some levity, he added, "Besides him breathing a sigh of relief for me getting out of high school, that was the proudest moment of our lifetime."

The Twins had a future Hall of Famer in Harmon Killebrew, and while they shared time at first base, Mincher became expendable. The Twins traded him to California for pitcher Dean Chance after the 1966 season. He became the Angels' full-time first baseman and finished in the top ten in the AL in homers, doubles, RBIs and average. But in the second game of the 1968 season, in a twi-night doubleheader, he was hit in the head by Cleveland fireballer Sam McDowell. Between the poor lighting and McDowell's velocity, Mincher never saw the pitch. "They didn't know whether I'd ever play ball again," he said. The pitch knocked out five teeth and did damage that led to hearing loss in his right ear and struggles at the plate, especially against lefthanders.

The Angels, believing Mincher was damaged goods, left him unprotected in the 1969 expansion draft, and the Seattle Pilots scooped him up. He made the All-Star team, but the Pilots swapped him to Oakland the next off-season, where he socked a career-high 27 homers. Early in 1971, Oakland sent him to Washington, and then the Senators became the Texas Rangers in 1972. The immortal Ted Williams was his manager. "We'd work on fundamentals in spring training, like hitting the cutoff man. The coaches would ask Ted what he wanted us to do and where to throw. He'd finally get so impatient, he'd go, 'Hell with all this. Let's go hit.'"

Needing a dependable left-handed hitter off the bench for their first pennant chase, Oakland reacquired Mincher in midseason.

Mincher more closely identified with the Twins than the other teams for which he played. When it was decided that Mincher should be portrayed by an actor in Huntsville's annual Maple Hill Cemetery Stroll, Pat Mincher requested the actor wear a Twins uniform.

When the 1965 Twins held a reunion, Don, Pat and fourteen family members flew to Minnesota, where, Don laughed, "They heard some stories I wish they hadn't heard." They went to a ball game, saw some old familiar sights and even went to the massive Mall of America. It sits in Bloomington, on the site of the old Metropolitan Stadium. They made sure to find a historic marker. A home plate is inlaid in the mall floor at the exact spot where it rested in the old stadium, where Mincher stood on the day he homered off a Hall of Famer in his first World Series at bat.

After his retirement from baseball, Mincher opened All Sports Trophies and spent time with the family he had missed so much during those long summers. Son Mark was a multisport star at Hazel Green High, a four-year letterman in baseball, football and basketball before signing to play baseball at Memphis State. Daughters Donna and Lori were hitting their teens.

Mincher refused one last offer from Charlie Finley to return to Oakland in 1973. There was this new position being created, Finley told him. Something called a "designated hitter." A perfect role for Don. "I thought it was the craziest rule I ever heard," Mincher would later say.

As Mincher was growing his trophy business in Huntsville, an ebullient coach in Nashville was building a reputation—and a pair of athletic programs. Larry Schmittou was head baseball coach at Vanderbilt, which he led to four consecutive division titles. Because college baseball provided little revenue, Schmittou's Vandy income also relied on his role as the head recruiter for the football team. With the school's high academic standards, the latter job was hardly a piece of cake, but the talent he helped assemble took Vanderbilt to its first bowl game in two decades. However, when a new director of athletics took over, Schmittou's football duties were eliminated. His pay went from $20,000 to $14,000.

Schmittou saw the success of Chattanooga's new team. "I thought if we got a park in Nashville, we could do even better than that." He left Vanderbilt and, with lifelong friend Farrell Owens, began the campaign for a new stadium and to land a Southern League franchise.

After a fifteen-year hiatus from pro ball, the Nashville Sounds became an instant success in 1978. Country music stars populated the park, and some even purchased shares. Schmittou promoted brilliantly. The stadium, longtime major leaguer and manager Buck Showalter said, "was like the Taj Mahal when we were there." Soon, Nashville became hungry for Triple A baseball. But, what to do about the Double A team?

Schmittou found his answer two hours to the south.

He met with Huntsville city leaders, including Mayor Joe Davis, and made his pitch for baseball. A new stadium would be built. The team would move there in 1985.

Following this with more than casual interest was Don Mincher. He ultimately he reached out to Schmittou to offer his services. Maybe he could be official scorer? Or handle the PA system?

Schmittou, as he usually did, had a better idea. The most famous name in Huntsville baseball should become general manager of the new team.

Mincher accepted the job, and Schmittou had a man who could open countless doors in Huntsville. And when Schmittou began pondering a sale of the club and potential move, Mincher helped gather a group of local owners to pool $7 million to buy the club and keep it in Huntsville. Mincher was named the Stars' president.

"He was Huntsville's 'Mr. Baseball,' and always will be," said John Pruett, former sports editor of the *Huntsville Times*. "He was the heart and soul of the Huntsville Stars."

Out of respect from fellow Southern League officers, Mincher was elected vice-president of the league in the late 1990s. Strictly an honorary position, he figured. Then in February 2000, league president Arnie Fielkow suddenly resigned to take a position with the New Orleans Saints. For a brief moment,

Mincher was stunned. Then he felt some relief, because Fielkow had been a polarizing figure. Finally, it sunk in: The vice-president has to assume the president's role.

Other league officials eventually convinced Mincher to delete the "interim" that had been placed in his title. With the blessing of fellow Stars owners, he put the Huntsville club up for sale. For nearly a dozen years, connected to the league office in Marietta by fax and email, he served as president of the Southern League until he stepped away in October 2011 as he dealt with poor health.

In December 2010, two and a half years before his death, Mincher got another surprise. The Baseball Winter Meetings were coming to a close at the Walt Disney World Swan and Dolphin Resort with the annual banquet. Mincher tried to grab a seat near the back of the crowded ballroom, but Pat kept insisting they move closer to the front, where unbeknownst to Don a table had been reserved for them. It was like dragging a stubborn mule across a pasture. He kept bickering, to the point that Pat exclaimed, "Don, if you don't stop doing that, you're going to make me cry."

Mincher, you see, needed to be convenient to the dais for the moment later in the evening when he'd be crowned "King of Baseball," the highest award in minor-league ball. "The first thing I need to do," Mincher said, taking the microphone, "is apologize to my wife."

Over a less fancy meal a few years earlier, Mincher dove into some chicken fingers early one afternoon in a Huntsville restaurant. His companion was demanding some introspection from Mincher.

"I'm proud of my career, but I'd like to be recognized not only for what I did as a player, but doing other things in the game."

THE NO-BLING GUY: JIMMY KEY

There was even more magnified pomp and circumstance than usual, including a stoic brace of Marine honor guard members, resplendent in their dress blues, marching onto the Fulton County Stadium turf. In front, two Marines marched with the U.S. flag and the flag of the Marine Corps. Behind them, another carried a Canadian flag…upside down.

Though Toronto manager Cito Gaston had maintained that this first truly international World Series—the Blue Jays versus the Atlanta Braves in 1992—was "not a battle of two countries," suddenly, it was. An entire nation felt insulted and disrespected.

President George H.W. Bush was forced to issue an apology. The Marines rushed into PR crisis mode. Canadian companies quickly cranked out T-shirts with the maple leaf emblem properly displayed and the words, "This Side Up."

The Atlanta newspaper, never shy with its boosterism in those days, hadn't helped. It had already proclaimed in a headline, "Message to Toronto: This is OUR game." It conducted a poll, asking readers, "Do people in Toronto speak English?" (To which the great Montreal columnist Michael Farber retorted, "We've been asking the same question about Atlanta.")

So international tension was still crackling when, on October 21, 1992, after nine years in the majors, Huntsville native Jimmy Key finally had his first opportunity to pitch in a World Series. On the mound for Atlanta was a Xerox copy of Key, the future Hall of Famer Tom Glavine, another left-hander with impeccable control and poise. In the opposite dugout was the man who gave Key his first major-league start, Bobby Cox, who had managed the Blue Jays before coming to Atlanta.

Cox first saw Key's potential during spring training in 1984, when he was the last man assigned to the Blue Jays' final roster as exhibition season ended. After a season in the bullpen, Cox recognized that "Jimmy's cut out to be a starter" and moved him into the rotation. Smart move.

Key spent fifteen seasons in the majors, going 186-117 with a 3.51 career earned run average and 1,538 strikeouts (to only 686 walks in 2,592 innings). He pitched for the Blue Jays, Yankees and Orioles and had ten consecutive seasons of at least 12 victories. Key threw a pair of one-hitters, against the White Sox in 1986 and the Indians in 1993, and he was five times selected an American League All-Star.

Not long after his induction into the Alabama Sports Hall of Fame, Jimmy Key (*right*) returned to Huntsville and joined some other Hall of Famers, like Condredge Holloway (*left*) and former college basketball coach Sonny Smith (*second from right*), at Hampton Cove, 2009. *Courtesy Alabama Media Group.*

In 1991, with the All-Star Game at his home park in Toronto, Key threw a one-hit inning of relief in the third and picked up the win when Cal Ripken hit a two-run homer for the AL in the bottom of the third. Said Key, "Maybe 50 years from now I'll look back and say, hey, I got an All-Star win—and nobody will know the circumstances behind it."

Twice he was runner-up for the Cy Young Award (in 1987 to Roger Clemens and to David Cone in 1994), and twice *The Sporting News* named him "American League Pitcher of the Year."

Finding any evidence of that success in Key's Florida home would be a fruitless scavenger hunt. "You wouldn't even know I ever played or existed in baseball," he once said in an interview. "I don't have anything around me that says that. I'm not really flash. [Awards] are all individualistic stuff. The accomplishments are in my mind. I don't need to show it."

The two World Series rings? Never part of the daily ensemble. As he explained, "They're too big for me." Not size-wise. Just too gaudy. It's serious bling for a seriously nonbling guy.

You could tell that from watching Key, who starred at Butler High School and then later at Clemson University. He was the epitome of the crafty left-hander, with finesse and guile, control and intelligence. As his former manager Gene Michael once told the *New York Times*, Key is "the best control pitcher in the game. When you think about an artist painting a picture or a genius on the mound, he is it. Obviously, he's smarter than the hitters."

It's what was instilled in him at an early age. It's what carried him through fifteen major-league seasons.

His first coach was his father, Ray, who passed away in June 2009, only a few weeks after Jimmy was enshrined into the Alabama Sports Hall of Fame. Key was actually right-handed, at least as a hitter and with his handwriting, but he learned to pitch left-handed. But even the simplest games of catch with Ray had a purpose. He was to throw to a target, not merely lobbing back and forth. Ray would hold the glove down and to the right, and Jimmy would aim there. Up and to the left, aim there. Chest-high, waist-high, whatever. And years later, in the midst of his career peak, Jimmy would say, "I just remember, whatever my dad told me, I did." And he was still doing it in the majors.

What he did in the majors he did in youth league ball. When he was twelve, Key pitched the title-clinching game in the Alabama State Little League Tournament, helping the team advance to the regionals in St. Petersburg, Florida. He attended McDonnell Elementary and Stone Middle School before arriving at Butler, where he played baseball, basketball and golf. He was part of a city championship basketball team that reached the state semifinals and led Butler to the regional title in baseball. As a senior, Key was 10-0 with 9 shutouts and a 0.30 ERA, batting .410 with 11 homers and 35 RBIs.

Key signed with Clemson, where he started the opening game of the College World Series as a freshman. He was the only player in school history to be All-ACC at two positions in the same season, as a pitcher and DH his junior year when he went 9-3 with a 2.79 ERA and 7 complete games, and a .359 batting average with 21 doubles. (For all his hitting prowess in preps and college, Key was 0-for-3 at the plate in the majors, playing his entire career in the American League with its designated hitter rule.)

Equal parts superstitious and loyal alum, he wore a Clemson T-shirt under his uniform for the two World Series wins in '92 and even convinced some Toronto teammates to do the same.

On the occasion of his first World Series victory, it was bitterly cold outside SkyDome, well below freezing on that late October evening. Inside among the 52,090 spectators was Brian Mulroney, the prime minister of Canada, and the "it couple" who then were what passed as American royalty, Ted Turner and Jane Fonda. The flag controversy aside, there was much common ground, beyond even the two managers, Gaston and Cox. Both teams relied on superb starting pitching—62 wins among the Blue Jays' rotation, 61 among the Braves' rotation—and had superstar talent, like Roberto Alomar, Dave Winfield and Joe Carter for Toronto and David Justice and Terry Pendleton for Atlanta. Both teams had deep benches and unsung heroes. Remember Francisco Cabrera and the RBI single to score Sid Bream?

Otis Nixon singled to lead off the game against Key. Uh-oh. As good as a double. Except Nixon got too bold and got picked off base. Then Jeff Blauser singled and stole second. But Pendleton lined to short, and Lonnie Smith grounded out to end the inning. The next four innings, Key paralyzed the Braves with his accuracy and mixing speeds. He retired 20 of 21 batters in one stretch, allowing only a harmless sixth-inning, two-out single to Nixon. After allowing a pair of hits in the eighth, Gaston went to the bullpen. The Toronto crowd was deafening in its ovation for Key. Uncharacteristically, he acknowledged the crowd by removing his cap and waving it.

It was the last time he walked off the Toronto mound in a home uniform. The *Ottawa Citizen* called it perfectly:

> *In what may have been his final start as a Blue Jay after nine classy seasons, Key gave us a game to remember. His five-hit, one-run* [in 7 1/3 innings] *gem could be worth a fortune on the free-agent market this winter.*

"It didn't cross my mind while I was pitching, but when I left the game I really thought about that. That's why I tipped my hat to the crowd. I usually don't do that but it was a special moment and I wanted to remember it."

It wasn't his final Blue Jay appearance, however. Key entered Game 6 in relief in the tenth inning (and had to bat in the eleventh) and was the pitcher of record when Dave Winfield, a .116 hitter in 43 previous World Series at bats, doubled in the game-winner against Charlie Leibrandt.

Indeed, the free-agency opportunity presented a substantial contract: four years, $17 million with the Yankees. Key went 18-6 and registered a league-best 17 wins in strike-shortened 1994 before arm surgery cost him most of 1995. Key was back in the World Series again in 1996, again facing the Braves.

He started Game 2, and the Braves chipped away at him for 4 runs while the Yankees were shut out by Greg Maddux. Down 0-2 in the Series, the Yankees rallied to win 4 straight games, with Key pitching the clincher in Game 6. It was his final game as a Yankee. Leery of his surgically repaired arm and his age, the Yankees wouldn't give him a two-year contract, so he signed as a free agent with Baltimore, starting 1997 with an 11-1 record before tailing off late in the season.

Key decided to retire following the 1998 season. Typically unceremoniously, the announcement was made through a prepared statement from the Orioles' PR department—Key again avoiding fanfare.

"I was very fortunate," Key said of his career. "It's very hard to get to that level. You've got to be at the right place at the right time. You've got to work hard. Nothing comes easy. The main thing was to be very fortunate enough, to be healthy enough to play that long, and lucky enough to be on good teams."

Michael Farber, the Montreal writer who so beautifully answered the Atlanta paper's volleys toward Canada, praised Key in a column, noting that he was "always pitching in the shadow of a Dave Stieb or Juan Guzman or (Jack) Morris or whoever was the flavor of the month. Sometimes," Farber said, "vanilla is taken for granted."

THE ACCIDENTAL ACE: CRAIG KIMBREL

From the sedan-sized stadium speakers come the first bold guitar licks from Ted Nugent. It is the beginning of "Stranglehold," a song that sounds angry and defiant and whose lyrics could never be mistaken for elegant, romantic poetry.

Huntsville-born Craig Kimbrel, shown in 2011, became a major-league relief ace. *Courtesy Alabama Media Group.*

But as Craig Kimbrel canters from the bullpen to the mound over the Nugent soundtrack, a game in the balance in the ninth inning, the sentiment of "Got you in a stranglehold baby" is not entirely inappropriate.

Kimbrel emerged as a devastating closer during a 2010 late-season call-up with the Atlanta Braves, launching a record-setting career. Kimbrel, who reached the 300-save plateau quicker than any reliever in baseball history, once prompted his former manager with the Red Sox, John Farrell, to tell *Sports Illustrated*, "Nothing is automatic, but Craig Kimbrel is darn close."

He was the National League Rookie of the Year in 2011, led the NL in saves his first four seasons in the majors and was an All-Star in seven of his first eight seasons.

"Stranglehold" would not be the appropriate soundtrack for the arc of Kimbrel's entire baseball career, which dates to the rec-league fields of east Huntsville, where opposing batters were loath to dig in deeply against a young pitcher whose relationship with the strike zone was an often fleeting one. He earned some amount of respect and attention, occasionally appearing in the newspaper after pitching exploits. Typically as not, the report added a second *l* to his last name. "After a while, we just laughed about it," Kimbrel would say of the misspellings.

It wasn't just Craig at Oak Park and Optimist Park. It was a family affair, also involving his two brothers. Craig "would be on the big field, Matt on the little field and Alan was on the T-ball field," recalls their mom, Sandy.

Kimbrel was a good, but not great, pitcher for coach Butch Weaver at Lee High School, not even a first-team All-City selection. (As Kimbrel emerged as a superstar, that fact was long used by colleagues to needle the sportswriter overseeing the team's selection.)

Then came one of those can't-make-this-up sagas. Kimbrel was selected to play in an All-Star Showcase game at Joe Davis Stadium in his hometown of Huntsville. He had pitched at the stadium before and had memories of going to Stars games as a kid. He was even there on one of the nights in 1994 when the Southern League was going gaga over that six-foot, six-inch, .202-hitting right fielder from Birmingham named Michael Jordan. At the Showcase, Kimbrel performed well enough to be "discovered" by Randy Putman, the head coach at Wallace State–Hanceville, a community college an hour away. He offered Kimbrel a scholarship after seeing Kimbrel pitch just one time.

Soon after, fate tapped Kimbrel on the shoulder. Or, more anatomically correct, it tapped him on the left foot. With hundreds of pounds of sheetrock.

Kimbrel's father, Mike, is an electrician, a free spirit with a fondness for motorcycles who has often taken cross-country trips on his bike to see his son pitch. Craig was helping Mike on the job one day in the summer of 2006 when a stack of sheetrock on a construction site tumbled over. Eight hundred pounds of material landed on Craig's foot, breaking numerous bones.

He was only two weeks from reporting to Wallace State.

Putman and Kimbrel devised a plan. While the rest of the team went through traditional workouts and a fall schedule, Kimbrel would continue to throw. From his knees.

The regimen built up arm strength, as well as more strength in his lower back. Kimbrel's velocity, once he was back on his feet, went from the eighties to the nineties. Pro scouts took notice. After Kimbrel went 8-0 as a freshman, the Braves drafted him in the thirty-third round. That's hardly "can't-miss" territory, so he returned to Wallace State for his sophomore season, striking out 123 batters in 81 innings. The Braves again picked him, this time thirty rounds higher. Kimbrel was the ninety-sixth player selected, forty-three spots ahead of his friend and former Lee teammate Buddy Boshers, who would go on to make 100 major-league appearances out of the bullpen for the Angels and Twins; Boshers joined the Twins in 2016, having resurrected his career with a stint in independent baseball and two seasons in Venezuela.

Both Kimbrel (no. 7) and Boshers (no. 40) had their jersey numbers retired at Lee, fulfilling a promise made by Weaver to honor any of his players who reached the majors. Such is Weaver's loyalty to his former players that he'd make dozens of trips a summer to see Kimbrel in Atlanta, and he made an all-night drive to Cleveland to be on hand for Boshers's MLB debut in 2013.

Despite that no. 7, Kimbrel's number of choice as a youngster was 10, in homage to a superstar whose poster hung on his bedroom wall. That was a poorly kept secret once Kimbrel reached the majors and became a teammate of that no. 10, Chipper Jones.

The Braves wisely saw Kimbrel's electrifying fastball and his mental makeup as ideal for a closer. Where the bullpen is often a demotion in the minor leagues, in Kimbrel's case, the assignment became a cornerstone on which to build. It didn't hurt that Atlanta already had in its stable another sub-six-footer with high-nineties velocity named Billy Wagner. A seven-time All-Star, Wagner had his own astonishing injury story. Twice as a youngster, he broke his right arm. So he learned how to pitch with his left hand. Kimbrel became Wagner 2.0 for the Braves.

Kimbrel was twice briefly promoted to the big leagues in 2010, then joined the Braves in September when the twenty-five-man roster was expanded. He finished 4-0 with an 0.44 ERA in 20 innings and even worked in the National League Division Series against the Giants. The legend truly became reality the next season, though Kimbrel's appearances were then accompanied by "Welcome to the Jungle" by Guns N' Roses. He faced 306 batters as a rookie, striking out 127. Only 48 managed a hit. That was the beginning of a stupendous four-year stretch with Atlanta, with 185 saves, 436 strikeouts of 1,039 batters faced and a 1.51 ERA.

He coupled a filthy hard slider with a fastball that was typically in the 97- to 98-mph range, though radar guns picked up a 101-mph fastball during the 2013 postseason. (There is a Huntsville tie to an even faster pitch. According to research for the movie *Fastball*, Aroldis Chapman, then with the Reds, delivered a 105.1-mph pitch to Tony Gwynn Jr., a former Huntsville Stars outfielder, on September 25, 2010, the fastest pitch ever recorded. "I didn't see it until the ball was behind me," Gwynn said. Six years later, former Stars shortstop J.J. Hardy was the victim of another 105.1-mph Chapman heater.)

Alas, the Braves were embarking on a rebuilding, austerity path. Atlanta reached the National League Division Series in 2013 after a 98-win season but fell to the Dodgers in four games. The latter was punctuated by a well-rested Kimbrel, stewing in the bullpen, as then-manager Fredi González refused to deviate from the norm and use Kimbrel in a nontraditional, one-inning save situation. Instead, the Dodgers tagged set-up man David Carpenter for a 2-run, game-deciding homer in the eighth. A gradual dismantling of the team began that postseason—an irony that catcher Brian McCann was left unsigned because of a youth movement but rejoined the team as a thirty-five-year-old before the 2019 season—and continued after a sub-.500 record in 2014. The Braves became a team with considerably fewer games in which a save was possible, and Kimbrel was a Ferrari used only for trips to the grocery store. On the eve of the 2015 season, Atlanta traded him to San Diego.

Nice weather. Fewer save opportunities. He pitched 61 times for a team that lost 90 games. Of the Padres' 72 victories, Kimbrel finished 53 of them, with 39 saves. By November 2015, he was swapped to the Red Sox. You can win a bar bet with the answer to this question? Who did Boston trade to obtain an All-Star reliever? Logan Allen, Carlos Asuaje, Javy Guerra and Manuel Margot.

Though his 2016 season was interrupted by minor knee surgery, Kimbrel was dazzling in 2017 with a 5-0 record, a 1.43 ERA, 35 saves and a strikeout of every other batter he faced. Free-swinging American League hitters hadn't seen the likes of what ex-teammate Tim Hudson called the "electric stuff" Kimbrel possesses. His encore in 2018 was a 5-1 mark, 42 saves—and his first appearance in a World Series.

It was a trying season in many ways for Kimbrel. Wife Ashley gave birth to their daughter, Lydia Joy, in November 2017. Lydia Joy was born with a heart condition and underwent surgery at four days of age. A second surgery would be necessary later that winter. A typical Kimbrel off-season of hunting, golf and relaxation with family back in Huntsville became a time of concern for his younger daughter, who was in the care of physicians in Boston. Craig missed three weeks of spring training as he remained with Ashley and Lydia Joy.

"She did a lot for me. A lot," Kimbrel told the *Boston Globe*. "Life changes when you have a child and the difficulties she went through, it definitely changes your view. It makes you stronger and makes you appreciate things more. It makes you appreciate each day more."

It was less than a year after Lydia Joy's birth that the Red Sox reached the World Series, where they defeated the Dodgers, 4 games to 1. Kimbrel, whose stats were skewed by an innocuous 2-run homer when the Sox enjoyed a 5-run lead, had a 9-pitch save in Game 2, threw a scoreless one and two-thirds innings in that historic eighteen-inning, 7:20 Game 3, then simply got to enjoy the view in the decisive Game 5, a Boston romp.

As the Red Sox celebrated on the Dodger Stadium infield, Kimbrel was easy to pick out in the crowd, with his long red beard and wearing a gray commemorative T-shirt over his game jersey. In his arms, a black bow around her head to block out the noise and wearing a pajama top with the no. 46 on the back, was Lydia Joy.

"I might have to remind her of that sometime," he said.

When the time comes, there's so much more, so many twists of fate, so many successes, that Lydia Joy needs to learn about her dad's stranglehold of the best hitters of the game.

KYLE WRIGHT

The thirty-five miles between Truist Park, home of the Atlanta Braves, and Coolray Field in Gwinnett County is a convenience. It's also a million miles away, it must sometimes feel.

Kyle Wright, the Braves' right-handed pitcher, knows the route well. He can probably attest that Atlanta traffic can turn those thirty-five miles into a three-hour tour.

Wright, a graduate of Buckhorn High School in Madison County, where he played for his father, Roger, led all major-league pitchers in victories in 2022 (21). He also collected Atlanta's lone postseason win, a 4–2 triumph on the eve of Wright's twenty-seventh birthday.

He was the seventh Atlanta Braves 20-game winner. You may have heard of a couple of others: Phil Niekro, John Smoltz, Greg Maddux and Tom Glavine. This after spending virtually all of the 2021 season those million miles away from the big leagues, toiling for Atlanta's Class AAA Gwinnett Stripers.

Wright was the fifth player selected in the 2017 draft and after one and a half seasons in the minors made his major-league debut in September 2018. He struggled in 11 appearances with the Braves in 2019 and was sent to Gwinnett. It was more of the same in 2020, but he was promoted in time to make the postseason roster. He threw six scoreless innings against Miami in the NLDS but suffered a disastrous loss in the NLCS against the Dodgers.

Except for two cameo starts for Atlanta in 2021, he was a Gwinnett Striper for the season and, by that point, a confused pitcher. Most effective with sinking fastballs and a filthy breaking pitch, Wright's delivery and style were tweaked. The proliferation of analysts and larger coaching staffs can be a blessing or a curse. What the collection of the Braves' brain trust didn't perceive and correct, Wright's college pitching coach at Vanderbilt, Scott Brown, finally did. According to a story in *The Athletic* by Andy McCullough, Brown thought Wright's delivery looked "manufactured" and called him.

"I could tell he was in a tough spot," Brown told McCullough. "He wasn't himself. He wasn't confident in himself. He hadn't hit rock bottom yet. But I think a year later, when he was in Triple A the whole year, he hit rock bottom. Realizing, like: 'Man, I'm so far from who I was.'"

The Braves had encouraged him to become more reliant on his two-seamer and breaking pitch and introduced him to Zach Sorenson, a mental performance coach. Still, he was back in Gwinnett in 2021 until a late-season promotion on the heels of a twenty-two-inning scoreless streak. Wright had two relief appearances in the World Series, striking out the side on 12 pitches in his first outing, then entering with a bases-loaded jam in the second, working his way out en route to an Atlanta win.

"I was like, 'I feel like I belong here,'" he told *The Athletic* about those games. Then, in 2022, he went on to prove that to the baseball world.

11
CUPS OF COFFEE AND MORE

*G*rant Dayton's Twitter introduction nicely sums up his baseball career and that of many of his peripatetic peers: "Seeing the states 1 baseball stadium at a time."

Dayton, a left-hander from Bob Jones High and Auburn University, is among a handful of Madison County natives who reached the major leagues but who didn't enjoy the longevity or stardom achieved by, say, Key and Kimbrel.

The list would include Buddy Boshers, Jed Bradley, Ken McBride, Stu Tate and Trey Wingenter. They have, like Dayton's intro, seen most of the states and stadiums among them, from Utah to Maryland, Mississippi to Washington.

McBride, the starting pitcher for the American League in the 1963 All-Star Game, joins this group with an asterisk dangling above. Though born in Huntsville, he was raised in Cleveland, Ohio—the site of that All-Star Game—where he was a two-sport star in high school. He signed a semipro baseball contract after graduation, then caught the eye of the Red Sox, who offered him a $500 bonus to sign. He toiled in the minors for five years until 1959, when the Red Sox sold him to the White Sox and he made his debut in the middle of a pennant race. McBride pitched seven years, twice leading the majors in hit-by-pitch, then became a Brewers' pitching coach before returning to Cleveland.

Imagine this: Your team is already getting whipped by the Dodgers, 7–0, in the third inning on one of those windy September nights at Candlestick Park, with the stands a third full of shivering, impatient Giants fans.

In the press box, there is a Giants official named Ralph Nelson, who signed you to your first pro contract and would thirty years later build a minor-league park in your backyard. Your manager, the redoubtable former pitcher Roger Craig, calls you to the mound for your first major-league appearance with a runner on second. Nerves, yeah. No wonder, after striking out Alfredo Griffin, you still uncork a wild pitch when facing Willie Randolph.

That was the scenario for Stu Tate on September 20, 1989, in his major-league debut. He had been on the scouts' radar as far back as his junior year at Hazel Green High, with a no-hitter among his eight wins. He signed with Calhoun Community College a decade before the Warhawks would sign a catcher named Jorge Posada, then went on to Auburn. The Giants drafted him in the eighth round, cultivated him through their farm system, then promoted him to the majors after being a Class AAA All-Star earlier in 1989.

Following the strikeout of Griffin, Randolph flew to center to end the inning. Tate then set the Dodgers down in order in the fourth and fifth, retiring, among others, the future Hall of Famer Eddie Murray. So excited were the few hardy fans, they began to chant "We want Stu!" as Craig removed him for a pinch-hitter.

Craig would call on Tate once more that September, in a losing effort against the Padres. Tate allowed a 2-run single on the last MLB pitch he threw. The Giants, on their way to a matchup with Oakland in the earthquake-delayed World Series, were pitching-rich. At spring training in 1990, his right shoulder was injured, ending his season and, effectively, his career.

It would be a stretch to suggest that Tate's attending Auburn was part of some sort of "pipeline" from north Alabama to the Plain, but there are frequent connections. Take, for instance, Hunter Morris, who chose to sign there in 2007 after the Red Sox made a miserly offer to their second-round pick out of Grissom High. Morris, who made it as far as Triple A in a seven-year pro career, became the SEC Player of the Year at Auburn in 2010 (ex–Huntsville Stars pitcher Tim Hudson won the same award thirteen years earlier). Morris then wrote one of the most astounding chapters in Stars' history, making a run at the Southern League Triple Crown and winning the MVP award in 2012 as the first Huntsville native to play for his hometown minor-league club.

The season Morris was SEC Player of the Year, Auburn had a second-team All-SEC pitcher named Grant Dayton, from Bob Jones High in Madison. The Marlins chose him in the eleventh round in 2010, starting that "1 stadium at a time" odyssey. Jamestown, New York. Greensboro, North

Carolina. Jacksonville, Florida. Jupiter, Florida. Phoenix. New Orleans. Oklahoma City. Tulsa. Finally, a 2015 trade sent Dayton to Los Angeles, and the Dodgers brought him to the show as an effective lefty set-up man in 2016 and 2017. As he was left unprotected by Los Angeles, the Braves picked him up on waivers that fall, but Tommy John surgery cost him the 2018 season. Then a promising 2019 was interrupted when he broke a toe on his right foot while playing catch in June.

Following Dayton from Bob Jones to Auburn to the majors is Anthony James "Trey" Wingenter, albeit with less hoopla. He was a gangly six feet, six inches at Bob Jones, just growing into his frame and gaining command. After Wingenter pitched three no-hitters in high school, the Mariners trolled a thirty-sixth-round selection his way after Wingenter finished at Bob Jones, so he opted for Auburn. There, as he once told *The Athletic*, "I was not any good in college." But a doggedly determined scout named Steve Moritz saw boundless potential and convinced the Padres to take Wingenter with the seventeenth-round pick. His arm strength and mechanics continued to improve. His velocity began to hit triple digits. Barely three months after he was drafted, he made his major-league debut on August 7, 2018, facing the Brewers' All-Star Lorenzo Cain—whom a teenaged Wingenter could have seen play eight years earlier as a Huntsville Stars outfielder.

When Grant Dayton joined the Braves organization, he was connected to another Madison County native with a saga on the opposite end of the spectrum from Wingenter.

Kyle Wright, a six-foot, four-inch right-hander, played at Buckhorn High and was something of a second-generation star. His father, Roger, was an All-City pitcher at Lee, in the generation sandwiched between the Holloway era and the Kimbrel era. He played collegiately at Calhoun and North Alabama, then became a coach. The ace of his final Buckhorn team: his son, Kyle. After being part of three College World Series teams in four years at Vanderbilt, Kyle was drafted fifth by the Braves in 2017, pocketing a $7 million bonus. After a mere 36 minor-league appearances, the Braves brought him to the majors for his debut in September 2018, with two hitless innings against the Red Sox.

Wright opened the 2019 season with Atlanta and struggled. However, in midseason, the Braves reached down to Triple A Gwinnett and briefly brought Wright back to the majors. The player they sent down to create the roster spot? Why, Grant Dayton, of course.

Two years after Hunter Morris's sensational year with the Stars, Jed Bradley became the next native son to join the team. He was born in

Huntsville, but the family moved around before resettling in Alabama in time for Bradley's senior year at Huntsville High. Despite missing much of the year because of an appendectomy, he was awarded a scholarship to Georgia Tech after a recommendation from a Huntsville High coach. Bradley blossomed into a first-round draft pick of the Brewers, made his Huntsville debut on June 3, 2014, but had several health issues and never met Milwaukee's expectations. He was swapped to Atlanta in an under-the-radar deal two years later, and something magical seemed to happen. On September 3, 2016, Bradley made his major-league debut, pitching a perfect ninth inning against the Phillies. Said Bradley to reporters, "I'm still trying to wrap my head around that whole deal." After announcing his retirement in 2017, Bradley returned to the game, in an independent league, in 2019.

Buddy Boshers could relate to the ups and downs of Bradley, and to Dayton's seeing all the states—and other countries, too. Boshers was part of a pretty fair one-two pitching punch for Butch Weaver at Lee High School, alongside Kimbrel. Boshers, who signed with Calhoun, was a fourth-round pick of the Angels in June 2008, just thirty-nine spots after the Braves chose Kimbrel. Boshers was promoted to the majors by the Angels for the last six weeks of the 2013 season.

Alas, Boshers wound up back in the purgatory of the minors, then as a free agent. There were two winters in Venezuela, then a year in independent ball before the Twins kept him busy as a set-up man in 2016 and 2017. The Reds released him during spring training in 2019, but after four games in the Mexican League, Toronto scooped him up, and he completed the 2019 season in the Blue Jays' bullpen.

For all of their accomplishments, the aforementioned gentlemen pale in comparison to Huntsville's greatest baseball prospect, a man who never reached the major leagues.

Condredge Holloway, still the consensus choice as the area's best all-around athlete, was an absurdly quick and gifted shortstop at Lee High School in the late 1960s and early 1970s and a fixture on the local teams that competed in national tournaments, teams that also featured future minor leaguers like Randy Davidson, Ron McNeely and Danny Parks. (Parks is, as he has noted, "the answer to a trivia question." While pitching for Pawtucket, he was the starter and worked six innings in the legendary thirty-three-inning 1981 Pawtucket-Rochester game that is the longest in baseball history.)

One day, Holloway welcomed a visitor to his office at the University of Tennessee, where an orange no. 7 tear-away jersey in tatters hung on his wall. "Are you the type," he was asked, "who could just pick up a Ping-Pong paddle or a pool cue for the first time and immediately be good at it?" Almost sheepishly, Holloway uttered, "Yeah."

He could have played college basketball. But baseball was his first love. As former Tennessee coach Bill Battle said, "We recruited harder against baseball than we did against Alabama or Auburn or anybody else." The Montreal Expos drafted Holloway fourth overall, behind Danny Goodwin, Jay Franklin and Tommy Bianco, ahead of such future stars as Frank Tanana, Jim Rice and Rick Rhoden, and a couple of young soon-to-be-transformed shortstops who went back to back in the second round, George Brett and Mike Schmidt.

Despite Montreal's eye-popping $100,000 bonus offer, Dorothy Holloway wasn't swayed. One of the first Black employees at Marshall Space Flight Center, Dorothy was determined that her son would attend college. Because her son was only seventeen, he couldn't sign the contract without her also signing, and that wasn't going to happen.

Condredge was highly recruited in football, and among his suitors was Paul "Bear" Bryant at Alabama. To this day, Holloway remains grateful for Bryant's candor. In the early 1970s, Bryant admitted to Holloway that the University of Alabama wasn't ready for a Black quarterback. That's why—along with the persistence of the Volunteers' coaching staff and the insistence of a determined mother—one of Huntsville's greatest baseball players instead went to Tennessee and became the first Black quarterback to start a game in the Southeastern Conference. That launched Holloway toward a Hall of Fame career in the Canadian Football League.

There is this important footnote: Bill Battle couldn't fully win the recruiting tug-of-war with baseball. He permitted Holloway to play on the UT baseball team, where he played alongside future major-league pitcher and coach Rick Honeycutt—and where Holloway was named an All-America shortstop in 1975. That's a couple of years after George Brett and Mike Schmidt made their big-league debuts and when the Expos were employing a career .251 hitter named Tim Foli as their shortstop instead of Condredge Holloway.

Ah, the road not taken.

12

THE FUNERAL DIRECTOR
AND THE NEGRO LEAGUES

*P*resident Lyndon B. Johnson was, according to Senator John Sparkman, "madder than hell" on that winter day in 1964. Huntsville's burgeoning role in NASA and space exploration was being threatened because of the strict segregationist policies of Governor George Wallace and the reluctance of Black potential employees to move to the city. Something had to be done, Johnson demanded, or Huntsville would lose its place at the table when it came to NASA.

Sparkman shared that information with Milton Cummings, who had entered the aerospace business after making a fortune in cotton and who was then serving as chairman of Brown Engineering. Cummings then called Woody Anderson, the prominent car dealer and a good friend. Cummings stressed that how this was handled "is going to chart the growth of Huntsville," as Anderson recalled in a letter to writer and editor Bob Ward in 1997.

While Huntsville had avoided the violence and ugly headlines that plagued so many cities in the region, it remained segregated. The racial divide was evident. Something had to be done.

Anderson was president of the Kings Inn Hotel, a 180-room property on North Memorial Parkway that had a secret button at the front desk. Whenever a prospective Black guest pulled up, the clerk would push the button to illuminate the "No Vacancy" sign outside. Cummings asked Anderson to allow integration at the property, but Anderson feared the reaction from customers and others in the city. Cummings met with his board of directors. They discussed various ideas for what Ward would call "gradual, no-fuss implementation" of integration.

Enter R.E. Nelms, a well-respected Black funeral home owner. Anderson approached Nelms to encourage him to eat at the previously all-white Kings Inn restaurant. Anderson met with the staff, then accompanied Nelms into the restaurant. Nelms ordered a steak that, Ward reported, was "inedible." Anderson personally entered the kitchen, had a steak prepared properly—and also threatened to cancel the restaurant's lease.

"Pretty soon," Anderson said in the interview, "the restaurant was serving everybody." The Kings Inn began accepting Black guests. Word reached the White House. Integration may have moved slowly in Huntsville, but it also moved with few violent incidents. More Black workers joined the NASA workforce. As Anderson told Ward, "You wouldn't believe in a hundred years that it could happen in Alabama in 1964 and not have a lot of bloodshed."

In 1951, Nelms had handled the funeral for the young wife of a Meridianville sharecropper who left behind a twelve-year-old son. When the youngster, one of six brothers, found his way into town, he'd stop to visit Nelms. Not only did Nelms have his mortuary, he also was something of a sportsman. He coached the Moore's Mill Red Sox, and the kid friends called "Pee Wee" joined the team as an infielder as a fourteen-year-old. Things were going well enough until a ball hit him between the eyes and he was transformed into a pitcher.

That worked out fairly well.

Eugene Scruggs blossomed as a pitcher. And, unsurprisingly, R.E. Nelms had some connections in higher places, including a relationship with Ted Rasberry, one of the signature figures in Negro League baseball. Nelms recommended Scruggs to Rasberry, who, among other ventures, owned the storied Kansas City Monarchs.

Scruggs became one of three Huntsville natives to play in the Negro Leagues, along with Carl Holden and Otha Bailey. Scruggs pitched for the Detroit Stars and Kansas City Monarchs in 1957–58. Holden was a catcher for the Birmingham Black Barons in 1960. Bailey was a catcher for ten seasons for numerous teams.

Theirs was a difficult existence. Hot, undependable buses that wheezed from town to town, often to places where the reception was inhospitable at best. Rooms in boardinghouses in segregated areas. Fields that were often little more than pasture, some even without fences. Paychecks far below what their big-league counterparts were making.

"It wasn't about money," Holden told former *Huntsville Times* sports editor John Pruett. "It was about traveling around, seeing new places. But most of all, it was about playing baseball. At that age, you're full of energy. Most of us were like kids being turned loose in a candy store. If you had a place to stay and good competition, that was all you wanted."

Nonetheless, they enjoyed a loyal fan base. As Scruggs told Pruett, "It depended on where you were. At the East-West All-Star Game in Chicago, we'd draw 40,000 or 50,000 at old Comiskey Park. We also played to some good crowds at big-league parks in Detroit, Kansas City, Washington. But sometimes, the best crowds were in the smaller towns. We also had good crowds in places like Nashville, Birmingham and at Optimist Park in Huntsville."

Eugene Scruggs—often recorded in Negro League lore as Dick Scruggs, having inherited an uncle's name early in life—was gifted with a sizzling fastball and a curveball described as "funky," though as a nineteen-year-old precocious professional with only five years of pitching experience, he sometimes struggled with his control.

Scruggs went to Grand Rapids, Michigan, to launch his career and was soon signed by the Detroit Stars, one of the Negro Leagues' premier franchises, and also spent time with the legendary Monarchs. Both clubs were owned by Rasberry, who was also a player-manager. Scruggs was a quality, middle-of-the-rotation pitcher. However, the Negro Leagues' days were obviously numbered as what had been a glacial pace of integration by Major League Baseball became more robust. And Scruggs was not quite the prospect MLB was seeking.

In 1960, Scruggs was a no-show at the Monarchs' spring training camp in Jacksonville. He had grown disillusioned and pessimistic about his chances to make the majors. He had trepidation about some of the travel. He was married, and he and wife Ethel had two children. Since he had no telephone, Rasberry couldn't reach him, so Rasberry and none other than the immortal Satchel Paige drove north to Meridianville to convince Scruggs to change his mind. They could never track him down in the rural community.

"I knew if I'd been there, they'd have talked me into going back, and I knew I needed to be home to care for my family," Scruggs told Pruett. It would be weeks later, when the Monarchs barnstormed north and played at Optimist Park, that Rasberry and Scruggs met. There was no changing his mind. And, indeed, Negro League baseball would soon dissolve.

Carl Holden, four years younger than Scruggs, was a multisport star at Huntsville's Councill High School, a Black school named for the founder of Alabama A&M University. Holden, in fact, played a season of football at A&M before a knee injury. A tryout with the Baltimore Orioles led to a modest contract offer, but only if Holden would agree to knee surgery. He balked at that and returned to Huntsville.

Again, enter R.E. Nelms. He convinced Holden to try out for the Birmingham Black Barons in 1960, and Holden made the club, playing that season and part of 1961.

Holden, like Scruggs, was a victim of timing. As he was peaking, the Negro Leagues were fading. But the pro baseball landscape was still not as welcoming. As Scruggs once told Rasberry, "Black players are having to play twice as well as white players to get to the majors."

Holden played a role in a one-hit wonder Negro Leagues saga. Horace Moore was an old friend and teammate of Holden, but Moore opted to accept a job at the airport rather than pursue an athletic career. As Holden and the Black Barons traveled to Huntsville to face the Monarchs in a game at Optimist Park, Holden began talking his old friend up to manager Jim Canada. Before the game, Canada sought out Moore, who, urged by Holden, had brought his spikes and glove to the game. Canada offered Moore, a left-handed pitcher, the opportunity to start.

Moore was pitching well through six innings until a Monarchs' slugger came to the plate and Holden called for a curve ball. "Let's just say it was a hanging curve," Moore would tell Pruett. "The last time anybody saw that ball, it was bouncing in the street on Oakwood Avenue. That thing may still be going.'"

Still, as Moore said, "I can truthfully tell people that I once pitched for the Black Barons." He continued, "I don't have to tell 'em it was just one game—and I don't have to tell 'em about that home run."

Like Scruggs, Holden continued to play baseball, joining some of Huntsville's amateur-league teams, and they both served as active Negro League alumni.

Ironically, Holden's predecessor at Black Barons catcher was another Huntsville native, the squat-figured, five-foot, seven-inch Otha Bailey. Though he had a solid bat and was gifted with great quickness, Bailey's size worked against him when big-league clubs scouted him. He had pride in having caught three no-hitters—and he also caught Pride. That would be a right-hander from Sledge, Mississippi, named Charley Pride, who had to settle for a Country Music Hall of Fame career as a singer once his days with the Black Barons and Memphis Red Sox came to a close.

Bailey spent his post-career life in Birmingham, where he died in 2013 after working in the steel mills and as a car salesman. Holden, who owned a beverage store with his wife, Hattie, died in Huntsville in 2015.

Eugene Scruggs celebrated his eighty-first birthday in the summer of 2019 and still works on occasion. Since 1975, he's been a licensed mortician and has been on staff at the Huntsville funeral home that still bears the name of R.E. Nelms.

SELECTED BIBLIOGRAPHY

Websites

Alabama Media Group. AL.com
Alabama Sports Hall of Fame. Ashof.com.
Anniston Star. Annistonstar.com
The Athletic. Theathletic.com
Ballpark Digest. Ballparkdigest.com
Baseball Reference. baseball-reference.com
Huntsville-Madison County Sports Hall of Fame. Hscshof.com
Newspapers.com.
Society for American Baseball Research. Sabr.org

Newspapers and Periodicals

Anniston Star
Arizona Republic
Atlanta Constitution
Atlanta Journal
Boston Globe
Chattanooga News-Free Press
Chattanooga Times
Decatur Daily

Gadsden Daily Times
Huntsville Mercury
Huntsville News
Huntsville Times
Los Angeles Times
Madison Record
Minneapolis Star Tribune
Mobile Register
Montgomery Advertiser
Montreal Gazette
Oakland Tribune
Orange County Register
Ottawa Citizen
San Francisco Chronicle
San Francisco Examiner
The Sporting News
Sports Illustrated
St. Louis Post-Dispatch
Washington Herald
Washington Post
Washington Times

Books

Golenbock, Peter. *Fenway. An Unexpurgated History of the Boston Red Sox*. New York: G.P. Putman, 1992.

McCarter, Mark. *Never a Bad Game: 50 Years of the Southern League*. Madison, WI: August Publications, 2014.

———. *Pandamonium: Inside Pro Baseball's Return to the Rocket City*. Madison, WI: August Publications, 2022.

Rankin, John. *Memories of Madison by John Rankin*. Virginia Beach, VA: Donning Company, 2007.

Interviews

Among those generous with their time in my reporting the history of the Huntsville Stars and Huntsville baseball history were Lori Webb—the successor to my holy trinity of Southern League presidents, Billy Hitchcock, Jimmy Bragan and Don Mincher—Craig Kimbrel, Jimmy Key, Hunter Morris, Gord Ash, Darnell Coles, Bryan Dingo, Cliff Pate, Darrell Evans, Keith Lieppman, Condredge Holloway, Pat O'Conner, Buck Rogers, Ralph Nelson, Buddy Boshers, Don Money, Paul Gattis, John Pruett, Rick Davis, Don Rizzardi, Steve Connelly, Tommy Battle, Paul Finley, Curt Bloom, Steve Kornya, Miles Prentice, Jay Bell, Aaron Cheris, Lindsey Knupp and Garrett Fahrmann.

The *Huntsville Times*, for which I typed for seventeen years, was an extremely valuable resource. Thanks to my old friend and colleague Paul Gattis for excavating some old stories from the archives, for being a sounding board on this project and for his coverage of the whole Trash Pandas saga.

ABOUT THE AUTHOR

*M*ark McCarter was the sixth sportswriter presented with the prestigious Mel Allen Award for "lifetime contribution to sport" by the Alabama Sports Hall of Fame. A four-time Alabama Sports Writer of the Year by the National Sports Media Association, he was inducted into the Alabama Sports Writers Hall of Fame in 2022 and named one of the "50 Legends" of the organization.

He covered the saga of professional baseball in Huntsville for seventeen years for the *Huntsville Times*, having previously worked for the *Chattanooga News-Free Press* and the *Anniston Star*. His work has been published in *Sports Illustrated*, *Fortune*, *The Sporting News* and numerous newspapers across the country.

He is the author of three previous books: *The Racetracks Book* (*The Sporting News*), *Never a Bad Game: 50 Years of the Southern League* (August Publications) and *Pandamonium: Inside Pro Baseball's Return to the Rocket City* (August Publications).

McCarter lives in Huntsville with his wife, Patricia. Since October 2021, he has been assistant athletic director for external operations at the University of Alabama in Huntsville.